FISHING FOREVER

Other books by David Churchill

It, Us and the Others

The Silbury Triangle

Not My World

A Focus for Writing

David Churchill was born ages ago in Swindon, where he still lives. He's really grateful to his grown-up daughter and son, Alison and Jon, whose combined efforts taught him how to use his computer the right way up. After over thirty years of enjoyable teaching he now leads patients in creative writing in the local hospice, walks miles on the hills with his wife Jaci, fishes the Upper Thames and Bristol Avon, gardens, and finds every excuse to be part of the landscape. He thinks his books write themselves when he's not looking, and he hopes they go on doing it.

FISHING FOREVER

David Churchill

Illustrations by Tony Whieldon

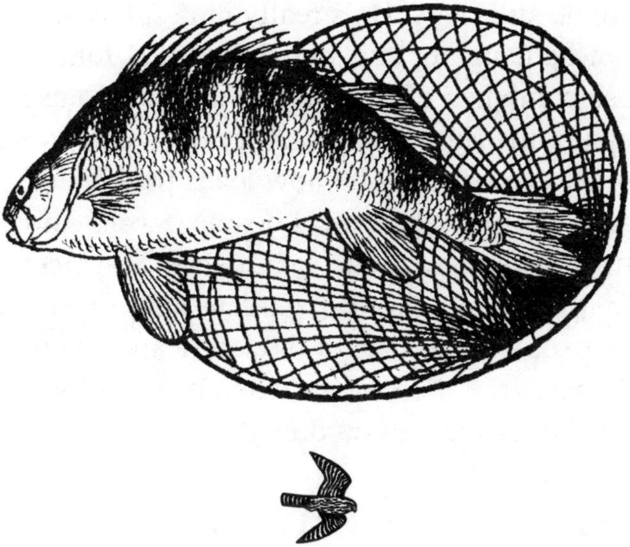

Merlin Unwin Books

Published by:
Merlin Unwin Books
Palmers House
7 Corve Street, Ludlow
Shropshire SY8 1DB. U.K.
Tel: 01584 877456 Fax: 01584 877457

ISBN 1 873674 406
British Library Catalogueing-in-Publication Data:
A catalogue record of this book is available from the British Library.

Typeset and produced by Merlin Unwin Books, Ludlow.
Printed and bound in Great Britain by Biddles Ltd.

Dedicated to everyone I have fished with, and with especial gratitude to Mike Jones and Ken Glasby who have contributed so much to my pleasure in the river and hence to these stories.

Contents

HOOKED

Friday and four o'clock at last. On the school bus. Big kids of Y11 ruling the back seats. First years at the front, excited about their homework. Me and Ken, somewhere in the middle, recovering from the stresses of the day.

Ken says, 'Come fishing tomorrow, Dave.'

'Not me,' I say.

'Give it a try. You'd like it.'

Ken's different from me. He doesn't say a lot, but it's hard to say no to him. Still, I have a go.

'I like football,' I say.

'Town aren't playing at home,' he says smartly. 'Go on, I've got no-one to go with.'

'You always go with your uncle.'

'Not any more. He's working abroad. It's a pain. Come on Dave. I've got loads of stuff you can use. We can make a day of it, if the weather's OK.'

I look out of the window, seeing the fields and trees whizz by, and a blood-red setting sun. Suddenly I quite fancy doing something different.

'You'll have to show me what to do,' I say.

The rest of the journey home I listen while Ken gets carried away about what we might catch, and how we'll do it. I've never heard him talk so much, and I haven't a clue what half of it means. I wonder what I've let myself in for...

Half past eight and I was still spooning down the muesli when Ken rang the bell. He paced up and down the kitchen while I packed up the sandwiches Mum had made and stuck them in the backpack that my homework usually lived in. Then we were on the road, me travelling light, but Ken well-loaded with a rod bag over his shoulder, a tackle box strapped on the back of his bike with elastics, and a folding stool on top of that.

It's a good job he was nearly six feet tall already – the biggest kid in Y9. On me, the rods would have been dragging the ground.

Soon we were out of the village and had turned off the main road.

'It's a brilliant day,' Ken said, sniffing the air. 'Great day for fishing.'

'Great day for football,' I said.

He ignored that. 'See where that belt of mist is lying,' he said. 'That's where the river is.'

In spite of all he was carrying he was going fast, and I had a job to keep up, especially with wellies on. I know now about the excitement that gets hold of you when you can almost smell the river, but it seemed a bit unnecessary at the time. After all, we did have the whole of the day – if I could stand it that long.

After a few more minutes we came to a bridge over a ditch, and a farm gate. I followed Ken off the road and we left our bikes chained to one of the gate posts. Ken unpacked the tackle box, and pushed the stool into my hands.

'You can carry that,' he ordered. 'It's for you to sit on.'

Then he was off at a great pace, over the humpy field, towards the mist. A bit of his unusual excitement was getting through to me now. It did feel good going somewhere I'd never been before, and the secrecy of the mist gave it a touch of magic. It was the fishing I wasn't so sure about.

After about five minutes of keeping up with Ken I was sweating in spite of the cold dampness of the air, but at last, after we'd gone from one field into another over a wobbly stile, there was a gurgling sound of water and he stopped and I could see that we were there.

'That's the River Ray,' he said, pointing to a smallish river coming in from our left, 'and this is the Thames.'

It was interesting to see how two rivers join. The little one came twisting out of the mist across the field, running through deep mud banks. Then suddenly the bank gave way to rushy beds, by where we were standing, and it flowed out into a wider river – the Thames itself.

Of course, it's not like it is in London. Where we live is near the start of the river, so it's only about as wide as a country road. But the water looked good, the way it curled and eddied as the two streams joined. Naturally, I felt like making a splash, so I picked up a stone and lobbed it in.

Before it even hit the water Ken was shouting, 'Dave!' He sounded really mad.

Whoops!

'Sorry,' I said. 'I forgot about the fish. Will it make a difference?'

'They'll get over it,' he said grumpily, after a moment. 'But move back a bit, and try not to wave your arms around so much. The water's too clear.'

I hadn't realised you can scare the fish away. First lesson!

I'll set you up with a float,' Ken said. 'The main river's only slow moving. You can fish along the side. I'll ledger in the hole where the rivers meet.'

I said, 'OK,' not having a clue what any of it meant, and still feeling a prat for lobbing the stone in.

A bit of bramble caught against my leg as I went to take an intelligent interest in what he was unpacking from his tackle box. I pulled my leg clear and stamped on the bramble to squash it into the mud.

'No!' Ken growled.

'What?' I said.

'Vibration – you've got a gift for it. Move quietly. I kicked a board on the edge of a lake once, and fish jumped out of the water about fifty metres away.'

I stood there like an idiot now, afraid to move at all. Did he really think this was better than watching football! At least you could make a noise without being told off.

Ken put a rod together that was twice as long as he was. Then he put a reel on it and pulled off line. I moved, carefully, a bit closer, and watched him thread the line up the rings. Then he pulled a good length through the top ring and did something to the reel.

'What did you do then?' I asked.

He showed me how the reel worked – how the bale arm traps the line and how you open it to get line off and how it snaps shut when you turn the handle. It was clever stuff.

'I'll put on a waggler,' he said. 'You'll manage better with a bit of weight.'

The waggler was a long, thin float, transparent, but with an orange tip. He threaded the line through the bottom of it and squeezed a big shot each side.

'Two AA's,' he explained, 'and a number 4 near the hook. It's three pound line. I'll tie it direct to a size 16 hook – barbless. Keep it simple.

It wasn't simple to me; more like a foreign language. Still, I was getting the general idea.

'We'll start about a metre deep,' he said, as he tied a little hook and snipped off the tail of line. 'If it's no good you can go deeper – 'til it drags the bottom. Perhaps a smaller hook.

The only fishing I'd ever done was for crabs, off the pier on holiday. The hook he'd used already was smaller than I thought existed. I couldn't see how you could hope to hook a fish with anything smaller. Unless all this fishing Ken did was only for really little fish, or tadpoles or something. But that certainly wasn't the way he talked about it. I'd have to wait and see.

'Now bait,' he said. He took the top off a round

green tub and I just managed not to jump back at the sight of a seething mass of wriggling maggots. I made myself peer closer. They were a mixture of colours – bronze and red – and they were all in furious movement, squirming and turning, like a thick liquid simmering in a pan.

Ken took an empty container out of his box and tipped some of the maggots into it.

'Right, these are yours,' he said. 'Chuck two or three in each time you cast, and put one or two on the hook. It's your turn to buy them next week.'

I opened my mouth to say, 'Who says I'm coming next week?' but Ken went on. 'Let's show you how to cast now, then I can set up myself.'

He fearlessly plucked a bronze maggot from the tub, nicked it on the hook and stepped to the edge of the bank. Taking his time – he's quite a good teacher, actually – he showed me how to hold the line against the rod with one finger, open the bale arm with the other hand, draw the rod back and flick it forward, taking your finger off the line so that the float can fly out, pulling off line as it goes, and land neatly out on the water. The float flipped upright and dipped under so that just the tip was showing.

'Now you shut the bale arm,' he said, 'take up the slack line and let the float drift around in that quiet water in front of you. I'll teach you trotting later on, OK?'

While I stood there, carefully holding the rod and watching the float turning gently amongst the bubbles and bits of straw, he was setting up his own rod, telling me what he was doing as he went. He was taking the teaching job really seriously.

'I'm going to ledger – bottom-fish – fish the tip,' he said. 'See this rod' – I glanced across, afraid to take my eye off my float. I didn't really know what I was supposed to be doing, but I wanted to get it right.

He was bending the yellow tip of the rod over, so far that I thought it would snap, but I could see how springy it was.

'No float,' he was explaining, 'just a weight that the line runs through, so the bait stays in one place right on the bottom. There's a deep patch where the waters join. I'm worming for perch.'

It didn't mean a thing, but I nodded and looked back to my float. It wasn't there. I looked all over the water in front of me; there were bubbles, bits of straw, a reed moving gently backwards and forwards – but no sign of a float. Now whose fault was that?

'Ken,' I said a bit nervously. 'Ken, my float seems to have gone.'

'Strike!' he said. 'Quick!'

'Strike...what do you – '

'Lift your rod. Now!'

So I jerked up the rod and out came the the float. It flew over my head and landed on the grass behind me. Not just the float though. A fish came too, flying through the air like a silver dart.

When Ken picked it up – I wasn't quite sure I wanted to – he said, 'It's only a bleak, but it's a fish Dave, they all count. Your first one, even if it did have to catch itself.'

He slipped the hook out of its lip, saying, 'Barbless hooks are great.' Then he offered it to me. 'You can put it back,' he said.

I cautiously held out my hand and he slid the shining little arrow into it. The fish lay there, panting, brilliantly silver, with one cold eye staring up at me.

'Go on then,' Ken said, 'it's had a bit of a rough time already,' so I swung my arm back to throw it into the river. Mistake number three!

'No.'

'No?'

'Don't throw it. Slip it in gently. How would you like it!'

Seeing the sense, I went to the edge of the bank, put my hand into the cool water and opened my fingers. It was really good, the way that fish took off back into the depths.

I turned to step up the bank and as I did, a lump of earth broke away under my foot. The clod of dirt, grass, stones, plus my left leg, went sloshing into the water – I nearly went too, but I just grabbed at the edge of the bank in time.

As I heaved up the side my welly boot, full of water, slid right off and splashed back in, all by itself this time.

There it was, half under the water, drifting slowly out of reach and on its way to London. I was just about to panic when Ken swept his landing net out and scooped it up.

'Well done Dave,' he said. 'What are you trying to do? Follow the fish?'

I was wishing I hadn't come, and thinking that Ken must be wishing the same. But he said, 'I haven't had a wellie-full for ages. Good job it's not freezing. Sort yourself out, then let's see if you can cast.'

It's not a nice feeling, wringing out a cold, soggy sock and dragging it back on your foot. Then sliding the whole chilly lot back into a smelly welly. I thought it might warm up inside eventually.

Still, I had caught a fish, and I quite fancied catching another.

So I managed to make myself hook a maggot on, and I pulled back the bale arm like Ken had shown me. The float immediately plunged down and tangled around a thistle.

After about five minutes I untangled it, wound

up the slack line and tried again. Again the line just fell off the reel.

I glanced at Ken. He was sitting comfortably on his box, his rod was on rests beside him, and he was contentedly watching the tip.

He felt me looking at him. 'What's up now?' he asked.

I told him. 'Try again. I'll watch...Hold the line first...With your finger.'

Ah! That's what I'd forgotten!

I held the line with my finger pressed against it, flicked back the bale arm, raised the rod over my head, and cast.

All that happened was that the float swung round and round the end of the rod into a tangle, with the float and the maggot somewhere in amongst it.

'You're supposed to take your finger off when you cast,' Ken said. 'Keep at it, everyone does that at first. And don't cast so hard next time or you'll end up on the other bank in amongst the cows. I've lost a lot of tackle that way.'

I was encouraged – and challenged. There was a lot to learn here, I reckoned. So I set about learning.

Two or three tangles and about half an hour later I managed a decent cast. This time I watched the float and when it dived under, after a moment of not being sure, I lifted the rod, carefully, and there was another bleak twisting and shaking on the end of the line.

This one dropped off before I could bring it in, but I began to feel that I knew what I was doing.

'You've got it,' Ken called. 'Wind in the slack line after you cast so that you can strike better. And if you keep getting bleak try moving the float up the line a few inches...fish deeper.'

So I fished, with one soggy foot but a feeling that I was starting to know what I was doing. After one terrific bite, when the float just dived, I hooked a little fish with a mouth as wide as its body, and tentacles under its chin.

The hook was further inside the fish's mouth and I was afraid of hurting it trying to get it out. Ken came over and showed me how to use a disgorger. He slid the slit down the line to the hook, gave a little push and twist and out it came.

'What is it?' I asked, as he went down to slip it back into the river.

'It's a gudgeon. They live on the river bed. Proper name is Gobio Gobio. Means it's got a big gob.'

He stepped down the bank to slide the fish back into the river, and as he bent, a movement over his shoulder caught my eye. It was the thin, yellow tip of his rod, twitching and bending.

'Look at your rod!' I shouted.

In two big steps he was up the bank. He took the rod off its rests and struck smartly

'Wow!' he exclaimed. 'What's this?'

It was definitely exciting. He was holding his rod up, as much as he could, but it was bending and jerking as if it was alive. What made it so exciting was knowing that something strong was on the end of the line, but not being able to see it.

Ken spared a moment to teach me.

'Look Dave – I'm loosening the clutch, so it won't snap the line. It's three pound line, but this fish has got a lot of power.'

He was slackening a knob on the back of the reel and there was a sudden scream as the fish took off up-river, tearing line off as it went.

'Got to keep some pressure on,' Ken said, 'or it might throw the hook. It feels like a big perch.'

He was winding line in, and sometimes the fish let him. Other times it went on a run and screamed off the line that he had just retrieved. But I could see how he was playing it, not forcing it. We still hadn't seen it, but it was definitely coming closer.

'It's getting tired now,' Ken said, after about five minutes of this. 'Get the landing net, Dave. Put it in the water ready.'

I did that, and he began to ease the fish closer to the bank. It was only making little runs now.

Then the line rose, drops of water spraying off it, and the ledger weight appeared. Then a tall spiky fin, like a sail, rose up, and a big scaly back with dark stripes running down it.

'Perch. Big perch,' Ken said, a bit croaky from the stress. 'Nearly there.'

The brilliant fish wallowed closer, and I saw my chance to net it. I lunged the net out to get under the fish, and several things happened at once.

One was Ken yelling, 'No!' Another was the fish leaping clear out of the water. And then there was a slapping sound as something snapped and the ledger weight flew through the air past my ear.

I looked at Ken. He was standing there with a rod that had no life in it, except for the slight bounce caused by the swinging weight.

What happened? I was thinking. What did I do?

'You great – ' Ken began, then he stopped. 'OK, it was my fault,' he said. 'I should have told you.'

'What...what did I do?' I asked. I felt terrible.

'It's all right,' he said. 'You weren't to know. You have to keep the net still until the fish is right over it. Or else it panics and makes a real lunge, like that one did. Trouble is, it's got the hook in it now. That's a pity. Perhaps we'll catch it again. They say the hooks come out. At least it's a barbless one, so it ought to. I've never caught a fish with a hook in, anyway.'

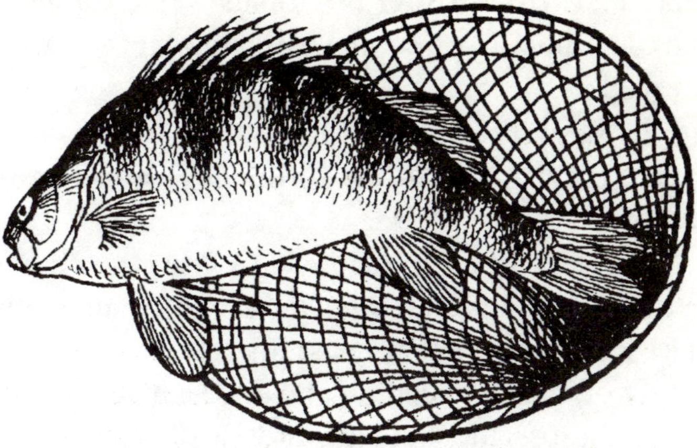

'Sorry Ken,' I said. 'I'll know next time. But I wish we'd seen it properly. Was it...something special?'

'Probably only about three pounds,' Ken said. 'But perch really fight hard. You can tell them by the big spiky dorsal fin, and the stripes. You have to hold them carefully or the spikes can make you bleed. It's a great fish. Try worms yourself and see if you can get one.'

So I changed to worms, and as time went on Ken caught half a dozen and even I had two. They weren't like that one of Ken's – only about eight or ten centimetres long – but they looked good and felt brilliant on the line. I spent more time in tangles than fishing and I knew I had a lot to learn. I must have wasted half a dozen of Ken's hooks and lots of shot, apart from losing two floats – one on the far bank and one in a tree downstream. All the same, I enjoyed it.

It was a nice place, there was a lot of skill to develop and I had all the different fish to learn to identify.

As the time passed, I saw a water vole swimming along under the bank, and an amazingly blue kingfisher swept past us several times. A family of swans glided by and once a heron flapped slowly across the field towards a distant bend. It was the first one I'd ever seen. Ken didn't talk much, but he gave me bits of information and advice and told me the names of the creatures. It was as if he was at home there, by the riverside. Even my left foot warmed up in the end.

By the time the light began to fade, and Ken said we'd have to pack up while we could still see, I knew I'd discovered something good – really good. I couldn't wait to come again, if he would put up with me.

As we plodded back across the field, towards our bikes – much slower than when we came – with the sun setting blood-red into the black trees, he said, 'What do you think? Coming again?'

'I will, if you've still got any tackle left,' I said. 'But I'll get some of my own. I'll be fourteen this month so there'll be birthday presents, and then it'll be Christmas. You can make me a list.'

'Do you know something,' he said, in a sort of satisfied way. 'I reckon you're hooked.'

He was right. I was. Forever!

SPOOKED

Line screamed off Ken's reel.

'Yes!' he shouted. 'It's on!'

His rod arched in a quivering bend. It was all he could do to keep it pointing up. A terrific swirl out in the middle of the river showed where a huge bream had surfaced then dived. Again the clutch shrieked.

At that moment my rod – well, the kid's rod, if you could call it a rod – was nearly ripped out of my hands. I was battling to keep control, and the kid was laughing, while something really powerful lunged on the line, and lunged again, desperate to force its way upriver.

And all this on the very next time we went fishing. But it wasn't only the fabulous fish that made it unforgettable. That evening, as the sun went down and the shadows spread across the fields, we had the weirdest experience of our lives.

We'd left our bikes up against a bit of old stone wall under a hawthorn bush, a field away from the river. It wasn't where the rivers join because Ken's Dad had bought a large-scale walking map of the area and Ken had spotted a place where there was an old right-of-way across the field to a bend of the river, below where we fished before. It was a bit further to cycle, but not so far to walk with all the stuff. You could hear the traffic on the by-pass, but it was a nice place.

We'd taken food and drink to stay all day and the weather was still quite mild and bright. I hadn't caught anything apart from a few trees and a lot of tangles, but I was getting the hang of it and enjoying myself.

Ken was ledgering worms on the river bed, and now and then his quiver tip would twitch and he'd strike. He'd caught two or three small perch but the fish didn't seem to be feeding much.

I was float fishing like last time, because I wanted to get really good at it, plus it gave me something active to do. I loved to see the float drifting and turning in the current, then reeling it in and casting again. It would bob a bit sometimes, but when I struck, the maggots were either chewed up or gone, and there was no fish.

It was about three o'clock when my float really disappeared and I struck like an expert. This time I knew there was something on the end. It was a great feeling as I brought it in.

I didn't need the landing net because it was only about four inches long, but it was a beautiful fish – bright silver and with pink fins.

'Well done Dave,' Ken said, when I held it up to show him. 'It's a little roach. Your first. Keep at it.'

I did keep at it, and I caught three more, all about the same size. I could feel the skill growing, now that I knew what to watch out for. But you really have to concentrate or the fish just suck the bait and zoom off before you can hook them.

Time passed happily and the sun was dropping towards the tops of the trees, when I suddenly had a feeling that someone was watching me. I looked over at Ken, but he was hunched up, concentrating on the yellow tip at the end of his rod. I looked behind, at the open field, but there was no-one there.

Thinking I was being stupid I turned back to the water, but that weird sensation soon came creeping up again. I tried to ignore it and concentrate on the fishing but it wouldn't go away. I even swung round quickly, but still there was nothing to see – nothing but the flat field and the distant line of the hedge. The feeling was so strong that it made me shiver. I was glad I wasn't by myself.

In spite of having the creeps, I caught another roach – a bit bigger this time. It was a great bite – the float went off on a slanting run before disappearing. I was just slipping the hook free when the fish jumped clean out of my hand, down onto the grass. In two flips of its tail it was over the edge and back in the river.

Ken called across, 'That one doesn't count,' and, right behind me, someone laughed.

Startled, I swung round.

It was a boy, about my own age, and I hadn't a clue where he had come from. I knew the field had been empty only a minute before. He had a fishing rod in his hand. His hair was long and brown and straggly and he was wearing a rough kind of brown jacket and shorts. He looked sunburned, like a gypsy. A sort of sack bag hung from his shoulder by a rope.

He grinned at us and Ken said, 'Hi'. I was too puzzled about how he had got there to speak for a moment.

The kid lifted his rod and said something but I didn't understand him. I saw his rod properly though. Well, it was a joke, because it was only a thin branch off a tree with a really thick line tied to it and a big hook on the end. He didn't have a reel or a float or anything.

While he studied the water. I looked across at Ken, to see what he was making of the kid, and Ken sort of jerked his head as if to say, 'He won't catch much!'

At that moment the water was glittering like jewels. Apart from the murmur the ripples made, a sudden quietness had come, as if we were miles and miles from roads or houses, but it didn't feel a bit creepy any more. I breathed in and the air had a minty, smoky smell to it.

The kid seemed pleased by what he could see in the water.

'The breams are to their suppers now,' he said.

I looked at him to see if he was being funny, but he was reaching into a side pocket in his jacket. What he took out looked like red hawthorn berries, of all things. He saw us staring and said, 'The grubs of the wasp are best, but I mislike the sting.'

He picked a berry and threaded the big hook through it. Then he gathered a couple of loops of line in his left hand and flicked the rod out over the water.

I've got to admit, he cast it as far as I'd been doing with Ken's good tackle. I watched the thick line curl out on that sparkling surface, then sink out of sight as the current took it.

It only seemed a minute before the end of his rod dipped sharply, and the line tightened. He let it slip through his fingers until the fish had taken it upstream, then he struck gently. We watched him play it carefully, just using his left hand to cushion the weight of the fish.

Soon he was drawing something really big and flapping towards the bank. When it was close in he put the rod on the grass, still keeping hold of the line, and slid down into the water. He grasped the fish behind its gills and scrambled back up beside us. I was a bit surprised to see that he had bare feet, but it was the fish that I stared at.

It was a monster – a gleaming monster. I had no idea that there were river fish like it. It would fill a school dinner tray.

'It is a bream!' Ken exclaimed. 'It must be more than six pounds. Fantastic!'

We crouched round the kid as he unhooked the fish, and watched him take a little round pebble from his pocket and strike it just once, on the back of its head.

I heard Ken draw in his breath to make a fuss, but the kid seemed so sure of what he was doing that he didn't speak.

The fish stopped flapping at once, and as it lay there in the grass I goggled at the size of it. It was brilliant silver with a great gold eye and fabulous fins. When we'd had a good look, and run a finger over the slimy, glowing curve of its body, he picked it up and slid it into his sack.

He looked at our gaping faces and laughed, then he cast again and in no time another fish, as big as the first, was sliding into his bag. One more, even bigger, and he put the rod down on the grass and squatted on his wet, bare heels as if the three he'd caught were enough.

'They're as fat as hogs,' he said in his odd way, rubbing his stomach. Then he dug a handful of berries out of his pocket and held them out to us. We thought it was rubbish bait ten minutes before, but now we took one each, said 'Thanks,' and rushed to get them stuck on our hooks. In fact I was in such a state that I ripped the little hook right off my line.

When he saw me scrabbling in Ken's bag to find another, the kid passed me his own rod. 'Use mine,' he said. 'You need no cork.'

I didn't know what he was on about, but now I grabbed the rod that I'd scorned before, stuck a berry on the hook and then made a mess of trying to cast.

He jumped up and showed me how he held loops in his other hand, just letting go at the last minute. I tried again and made a reasonable sort of job of it. Anyway, the moving water took the heavy line and carried it out, sinking, towards the fish.

Well, that river was teeming. The sun was

only just above the trees now and the surface of the water was melted gold. Over every inch of it fish were rising and rolling, the circles crossing each other as they spread from bank to bank.

The kid urged us on with quiet murmurs, and laughs, and bits of good advice, and we fished as if we'd never be able to fish again. And we caught as we'd probably never, ever catch again.

Ken was taking bream from the bottom that made his rod almost bend double and set the clutch screaming. And my line jerked to give me the most exciting ten minutes of my life, trying to manage the fish without breaking the rod or the line, copying how the kid had done it, until he was able to slide down the bank and lift out a golden-brown, torpedo-shaped beast with big scales and a giant mouth. Ken spared a second to look at it and say, 'Chub. Fantastic!' before seizing his own rod and getting back into the action.

It went on like that, hooking some and losing some, but always fabulous fish taking those berries. Ken was getting great use out of his landing net, and the kid was laughing and sliding up and down the bank to take out my catches and show me, before slipping them back in the river. I'd never had any idea that fishing could be so exciting.

Once there was an explosive surge at my very feet and a jagged-mouthed monster burst half out of the water to tear a fish clean off the end of my line. I jumped back in terror.

'Pike!' Ken exclaimed. 'A twenty pounder!'

'You did well to leap,' the kid said seriously. 'I knew a maid who was bit in the foot. But it's good to bake with onion in its belly.'

Ken raised his eyebrows at all that, but by then we were getting tuned in to the kid's weird speech. Anyway, he was great company and I reckoned he knew more than Ken about catching and handling fish – cooking them too. He was as excited as we were, as if he didn't often have someone else to fish with.

I hooked one that almost pulled me into the water until it calmed down a bit. It took ages to land. In the end the kid staggered up the bank with both arms wrapped round it. It looked like a giant version of a little Big Gob, with the same sort of feelers hanging from a mouth as big as a milk bottle top.

'Barbel! I've never had one of those. Brilliant!' Ken shouted across to us. The kid slid back down and held it in the water, resting it, until it was ready to thrash back into the flow. He really did know how to treat them – if they weren't for supper, that is!

After that I was so shaky from the excitement and the effort that I actually stopped fishing. I was just going to ask the kid if he wanted his rod back to do some more himself, when there was a call, a woman's voice, carrying clearly across the field in the calm air.

'Coo-ee!' And it came again, 'Coo-ee!'

At once he reached for the rod. 'Mother is looking out for me,' he said. 'I must go. But I'm often here.'

I didn't want him just to vanish, we'd been a great team and I really liked him.

'Where do you live?' I asked, more to delay him than wanting to know.

He pointed to the direction the voice had come. 'Yon small cot,' he said. Something like that, anyway.

I hadn't seen a cottage, if that was what he meant, but Ken said, 'OK, we'll pack up too. It'll soon be dark.'

But by then the kid had coiled his line, heaved the heavy bag onto his shoulder, and was heading away across the field, bare feet and all.

We started to take our stuff apart, still half in a dream from all the fish. But things were different somehow, once we were by ourselves. There was a bit of a chilly breeze and the air had lost its scent. In fact there seemed to be an almost disagreeable taste and smell to it. The water looked dull, and the fish weren't showing any more. A bird croaked, and that was it, apart from a growl of traffic from the by-pass.

As soon as we could, we set off back over the field. The sun was behind the branches of the trees, but we could see the dark trail of the kid's footsteps in the dewy grass.

'He was a bit weird,' Ken said, just as I was thinking the same thing. 'I mean – he was great, but he had bare feet, didn't he, and his tackle was rubbish. D'you reckon he was English?'

'He was a real country type,' I said, 'like talking to a foreigner. But he couldn't half fish...or was it luck? I mean, is it often like that?'

'No way,' Ken said. 'Well, I've never seen anything like it. You don't get fish like those – not so many. And the condition they were in! What did he say? "Fat as hogs," and they were!'

'Where's his house then?' I asked, as we passed through the open gate into the second field. 'It can't be far if he gets here without any shoes. I didn't see one by the road.'

'Just follow the footsteps,' Ken said, 'and you can't miss it.'

Well, the trail was going our way, so we tracked it, like Ken said. It went across the field, towards where we'd left our bikes behind the bit of old wall under the hawthorn. We were just coming up to it when the footsteps simply stopped. There was one clear wet footprint on a slab of stone, half covered by the grass, and then nothing more.

'That's funny,' I said. 'There aren't any houses here – I knew there weren't. Where's he gone? He can't just vanish.'

'He might,' Ken said. 'He was pretty old-fashioned with his "yon small cot"! Perhaps he was a ghost.'

It was a joke. Well, it started out as one, then suddenly it wasn't. The goose bumps ran up and down my arms so that I actually shuddered, as if someone had walked over my grave, as they say. Only it wasn't *my* grave that we found ourselves staring round anxiously for. I remembered how I'd been feeling before he appeared on the bank. And he did just appear, too.

I looked at Ken and he looked at me, and we didn't say a word. A last red ray from the sun came like a finger under the lower branches of the trees that had been hiding it. Suddenly I realised that Ken was staring past me, towards where we had left our bikes. And I knew he had seen something.

Half afraid to look, I followed his gaze.

I don't know what I expected. A gravestone? A skeleton? A monk without a head?

I didn't see anything like that, but what I did see prickled the hair on the back of my neck and turned my mouth as dry as sandpaper.

It was that last beam of sunlight that did it. What was in front of us was so obvious, yet we'd dumped our bikes and walked right out through it a few hours before, without any idea at all. It wouldn't have meant much to us then, anyway.

The red light, and the shadows it cast, were picking out all the traces. The stone slab with the footprint – fast drying now – the mossy stone blocks in the grass, in a sort of rectangle running off from the slab. The ruined bit of wall, with blackened stones at the bottom.

An eerie kind of half-light was seeping into the trees and bushes that grew where the walls had crumbled. At our feet was the doorstep, and the remains of the fireplace stuck up through the scrubby grass beyond. As we stared, the little cottage seemed almost to rebuild itself in front of our eyes.

There was a red stain of sunlight on the stones beside our bikes, as if a fire still glowed in the hearth. And the hawthorn berries above, reflected it back like sparks.

It was very, very spooky. Sweat trickled down the side of my face and I heard Ken mutter, 'Yon small cot,' but he wasn't laughing this time.

We just stood there, looking slowly round us. It took no effort to picture the walls in place, and a wooden door where the step was; a couple of small windows looking out into the woods...the fireplace...a wooden ceiling. I looked down to see if the rafters were still there in the grass, but they had all gone, rotted away into the earth, like the floor itself. It was wide open to the darkening sky, only overhanging branches where the roof beams used to be.

It was so easy to imagine a table and simple chairs, and people...a boy and his mother...sitting at the table. As we stood there, just drinking it in, I shivered. It was a good shiver, not fear, even though it ran all the way from the back of my neck right down to my feet.

But the light was fading, and the glow that had warmed the stones dimmed as we watched. Now there was no more to see than a bit of wall and some bushes. In another moment the glow had gone and real darkness was coming. Quietly, we unlocked our bikes, keeping a bit close and sort of tiptoeing, but still not exactly afraid. Then we wheeled out through the hedge and onto the road.

Cars went past with bright headlights, and the ordinary world began to claim us back.

'I don't believe in ghosts,' I said, making an effort.

'Nor did I,' Ken muttered. 'Come on, our mothers'll be looking out for us as well. It's getting really dark.'

We pedalled off but we didn't say much on the ride back, except when we were near home and Ken started to reckon up how many fish we'd caught and what the weight might have been. But it was too difficult to add up, and it was the other thing that was filling our minds anyway.

I was thinking, was he really a ghost – the ghost of a boy who used to fish that spot on the river? And if he was, could he possibly have brought his old world with him, wearing it, like a cloak or a bubble? Had we been breathing the air of years long past? And the river we fished – was that brilliant water flowing out of Time itself? And if that's how it was, what about the fish?

I mean, are they part of our river, or did they come swirling and shining from some distant time when air and water were pure, and boys went fishing barefoot across the quiet fields?

They felt real enough on the end of the line, and when we got home we still smelt so fishy that both our families held their noses. But it left such a spooky feeling that I didn't want to talk about it. I just pushed it down in my mind and I was glad that Ken didn't seem to want to talk about it either.

The fishing had been amazing, but next time, perhaps, we'd try somewhere different.

LANDED

'What if we get caught?'

'Who by?'

'Sodger'll want our absence notes.'

Ken didn't have a quick answer to that. I could just picture Sodger thrusting his chin across the table at us. Short black hair with a bald spot. Rimless glasses. Small black moustache. Very quiet voice, especially when he was really mad. Saying:

'You were both away yesterday. May I have your notes please.'

'No problem,' Ken said at last. 'I shall say, "Sorry Sodger, it was the last day of the season.

Fishing was more important than school." He'll understand.'

I didn't even laugh.

It was too late to worry anyway. We were on our way and there was no going back. The winter had come and gone and we'd fished when we could. Not where we met the kid, though. We'd definitely go there again – but not just yet. One reason was that we'd looked at the map and found an even shorter route to the river, down a farm lane. It came out higher upstream, but there were some good deep holes where the chub hung out, and streamy runs over the gravel. The sort of place where dace and roach lurk under the weed mats.

When Ken told me about the close season – no fishing for three long months while the fish are breeding – it was a shock. We'd missed enough chances to fish because of gales and floods, and snow in January and February. What started as a joke, the idea of us skiving school to fish Wednesday, the last day of the season, got really serious when it rained all weekend. It got so serious that we couldn't resist doing it, even though we'd never skived before.

So planning followed: clothes, tackle and maggots smuggled round to Ken's garden shed on Tuesday evening; me caught digging for worms and having to pretend I wanted to help with the weeding – I'll suffer for that!; round to Ken's at quarter past eight, after his parents had left for work; feeling as guilty as hell as I unpacked school books and loaded up the tackle; changing out of school uniform; waiting a bit – really nervous – until there were no other kids about, and then slipping away down the backways, quickly across the main road and turning left – different from usual because it cut down the chance of anyone recognizing us on their way into Swindon – down a side road that went past some old farm buildings, along a bumpy track, and we'd made it.

There was no sign of anyone else, apart from a car tucked away by some bushes. We put our bikes behind some more.

'We can just say our parents have rung the office,' Ken said. 'I don't suppose he checks.'

Knowing Sodger, I thought he definitely would check. But there was always a forged note, of course, if I dared. Except that he was probably a handwriting expert.

Meanwhile it was quiet, sunny, and the usual feverish feeling of excitement was overcoming my jumpiness and making me want to rush to the water and get started.

We crossed the field to the white wooden bridge and decided to go well down the river, just in case anyone local came across the footpath and recognised us.

At the second bend we stopped because we could see someone fishing about fifty metres further on – just a dark figure standing below the bank at the gravelly edge of the water. That explained the car.

Where we were, there was a deep hole in the river under a big willow, followed by a slow run, so it suited us well enough and we set up our tackle. Knowing that it was the last time for three months, I took a lot of care – of course, I'd learned a bit since last November.

Ken wanted to use a stick-float and trot the run, while I was going to ledger the hole.

I set up the quiver-tip rod that I'd had for Christmas, with a ledger stop holding a small bomb on the three pound line. I tied on a hook length of pound line and practised my latest skill, using a hook tier, to attach a spade-end size 18 hook. I baited up with two maggots and cast it out into the centre of the pool. Then I adjusted the height of two rod rests, exactly, and laid the rod gently on them. I slackened the tension of the line a little, threw in a sprinkle of maggots and sat down on the plastic bag that was the only seat I could bring.

School and Sodger were a niggle in the back of my mind, but I watched the rod tip and tried not to think about tomorrow.

Ken soon caught a decent dace – lovely long silver fish – and then another. The bites were very fast and he was doing well to connect with them. I had a twitch on the rod tip, only to find that my old mates, the gudgeon, were as hungry as ever. After catching five I decided to have a change. Patiently, I set up my thirteen-foot float rod – that was from my birthday – and a waggler.

Almost on the drop it plunged under. I played it carefully as it steamed around the pool and soon a chub of about a pound came gliding up into the landing net that Ken was holding steady in front of me. That was brilliant and it drove all thoughts of school clean out of my mind. I settled down to float-fish, sprinkling maggots in at the head of the pool and trotting the waggler across it.

Unfortunately, catching the chub seemed to have spooked the other fish and all I could contact after that was the occasional little silver bleak and – even worse – a couple of minnows. So I got restless and decided to give the pool a chance to settle while I tried one or two other spots nearby.

I wasn't as happy as I should have been. The chub was enough to have made it worth coming, but the thought of facing Sodger tomorrow was back in my mind. My parents would go mad if they found out I'd missed school. I'd be grounded for the rest of my teens.

It was dead quiet and I even had really stupid thoughts that something could happen to us and no-one would ever know. We had a Police talk in school last year about the dangers of skiving; it didn't mean much at the time.

I wandered along the bank, casting in here and there. As usually happens when I don't settle to one place it wasn't long before I wrapped the line round a piece of bramble. I cussed, gave a tug, and of course, snapped off the hook length.

That meant going back to tackle up again. I put my rod on the grass and slid down the low bank to stand by Ken on the gravel beach where he was fishing.

'Any luck?' I asked.

'No,' he said. 'No luck at all. Just skill. Three more dace and I hooked something really heavy, but it came off. Could have been a barbel. I'm going to bring luncheon meat next –'

What stopped him was a shout from down river. I jumped, thinking someone was yelling at us. We were both staring in the direction it had come from when there was another cry. There wasn't any doubt this time, though – it was a cry for help. More like a scream, but extra alarming because it was suddenly cut off.

We didn't stop to think. Ken pushed his rod up onto the bank and we scrambled after it and started running. There was no sign of the other person who had been there when we arrived and there were no more cries. But as we got closer I could see a black tackle box in the grass on the edge of the bank.

Side by side – Ken's big, but I'm quick – we came up to it and stopped, puzzled and panting, wondering where the bloke was. And then Ken said, 'There!' as something came up out of the river right in front of us. An arm, spraying water, waved violently in the air, followed by a bulge which revealed itself as the back of a human head plastered in weed. The arm flopped out over the gravel and a hand scrabbled and grasped at last year's dead rushes. They tore free and the head and the arm plunged under again, leaving a swirl in the water, and drifting bits of weed.

It was such a shocking sight that we froze for an instant. Then the arm came up again, but not so high. This time it was hardly on the bank before the clawing fingers scraped back down over the slimy stones and slithered into the darkness.

Now we moved fast, jumping down the bank and both ready to go in. As we hit the gravel, the head and a shoulder reappeared, drifting further out. Ken yelled, 'Keep hold of me!' and crouched, reaching as far as he could. I hung on to his other arm, trying to dig my heels in.

The bloke was fighting for his life – you could tell there was a struggle going on under the water – and his hand and wrist came up again through the weeds. It groped in our direction, still searching for something to hang on to. Very slowly it swung towards us, and there was an agonizing moment when it looked like disappearing again. Then he must have made one last desperate effort because the arm suddenly came quite high out of the water. Ken saw his chance and lunged for it, almost heaving us both over the brink.

'Got him!' he grunted.

I leaned back, my fingers gripping Ken's other arm, and we pulled. The body eased towards us, but still more or less under the water. There was an urgent need to get his head up into the air, but the weight was terrific with all the water in his clothes.

Once he was against the edge, I joined Ken and we took hold of a shoulder or arm each and began to heave him up on to the shore. I was afraid he was going to die and it was great when his face came free of the water.

It was a struggle and he weighed a ton, but slowly we dragged him out until half of him was lying clear. We paused for breath, and to dig our feet in again, still keeping hold, under his arms now. He lay there on his face, smothered in weed but definitely alive. As if to prove it, he started retching and choking and a stream of river water came heaving out of his mouth and into the gravel. At least we didn't have to do the kiss of life, or anything drastic like that.

Being sick did him good and now he began to try and help us, heaving and straining, grunting and gasping, levering himself on out of the water until he was completely clear. Then he rolled over and sat up, his head between his knees, fighting to steady his breathing.

He was plastered in mud and duckweed – the green stuff that floats like a mat on top of the water. We sat back on our heels feeling quite pleased with ourselves but a bit shocked and not knowing what we ought to do next.

After spluttering and spitting a bit more, he lifted his head and started to clear the weed off his face. What I thought was funny was that he still had glasses on, in spite of all the struggling. There were little round green leaves stuck on them and dangling down the ear pieces.

Then he cleared a bit more of the stuff off his face and passed his hands over the top of his head. The weed still stuck in amongst his spiky black hair, but a bald spot shone clear in the middle of it. He went on rubbing the mess off his nose and chin, revealing himself in a kind of slow motion.

As he did, my eyes began to switch frantically from the bald spot to the glasses, and down to the jutting chin. A crazy idea was taking me over. I thought I recognised him even though I desperately didn't want to. Then a blob of mud and weed was swept away to reveal a small black moustache, and there was no doubt. It was worse than a nightmare!

I had the urge to scramble up and run, while he was still trying to get the mess out of his eyes. I looked over him and met Ken's stare. There was a look of horror on his face. He was as rigid as I was. That made it worse. I wasn't imagining things. It was impossible, but it was horribly, horribly true.

Then the mud-smeared face turned in my direction, blinking and staring at me, wonderingly. I was still trying not to believe what I was seeing and it looked like he couldn't take it in either.

We stayed like that for a long, dreadful moment until at last he turned from me to Ken. A shivering cold chill was gripping my body and freezing my tongue. I felt like I was the one who had nearly drowned. In fact I felt as if I *was* drowning. There was a sort of strangled gulp from Ken, as though he was trying to say something but his mouth wouldn't work.

Sodger looked back at me. He ran a finger over his glasses, to make sure that he was seeing right. I could have told him he was, if my brain hadn't just dropped dead and left me paralysed.

In a croaky, doubtful kind of voice, he said, 'Kenneth York? And David Chappel? Oh dear!'

We both stayed dumb.

He went on, almost as if he was talking to himself.

'I had no idea it was so deep...the edge just broke under my feet...impossible to get out...waders full of water...weighed a ton...terrifying...thought I was gone...you saved my life!'

We'd saved his life all right. But what had we done to ours? And then I thought, Hey! What's he doing fishing anyway? Do teachers get days off like that? He should have been taking us for registration, and for English – if we'd been there.

He was getting his breath back now, and he went on, speaking more strongly, but still not like his old deadly self.

'I couldn't resist it, you see,' he said. 'It's the last day of the season. Did you know that? Yes, of course you did. Suddenly I couldn't bear to spend it in school. It's been a very hard year for all of us. I've never done it before, never. You must believe me –'

Ken found his voice then.

'Nor have we,' he said. 'Honest, Mr Southwood. We know how you felt – '

'Oh no you don't,' Sodger said fiercely.

'You're not a teacher. My need was greater than yours.'

He groaned, passing his hands over his messy hair, smearing fresh yellow mud across the bald spot.

'But I should never have given way, though. Never! Now I've got to get all this past my wife. What terrible luck that you two should be here. I shall have to resign. Think what those horrible little newspapers will make of it!'

He put his head in his hands and just sat there with his clothes oozing slimy mud and water. I didn't think it was quite fair to call us bad luck, not after what we'd just done, but for a minute, I actually felt sorry for him

'It's all right,' I heard myself say. 'We won't tell, will we.'

'No way,' Ken said.

After all, we'd saved his life. No point in wrecking it now.

He looked up at me, doubtfully, then he almost smiled. It was a bit horrible, mud and all, but the idea was there.

'Could you possibly bear to keep it to yourselves?' he asked. Then he nodded, causing fresh trickles of water to run down out of his hair. 'Yes, I think you two probably could. Well, I won't tell either – of course. That's the very least I owe you. Thank God you were here!'

He suddenly shuddered and went on shivering. He looked quite ill, or shocked, as if he was realising for the first time just how close to death he had been.

It was all a bit embarrassing but then Ken asked, 'Did you catch anything, sir?'

Sodger's expression changed at once.

'Oh yes,' he said, 'I was into some nice little roach. And I'd just had a terrific bite when the bank gave way. Where's my rod? Don't say I've lost it!'

But he must have thrown the rod clear as he did his dive into the water. It was lying on the gravel by Ken. Ken reached over and picked it up. As he did, it jerked down so sharply that it came clean out of his hand. Immediately, drawn by an invisible force, it began to slide away into the water.

Sodger tried to reach it, but his waterlogged waders kept him rooted to the spot. Ken went full length and clamped one of his big hands across the reel. Just in time.

'Land it! Land it!' Sodger was shouting, struggling to his feet. He was as mad as we were, you could see that.

Anyway, he let Ken play it, taking his time now because it was obvious that it was a really good fish.

'It must be a barbel,' Sodger was saying.

'Not as strong as that,' Ken said.

'Chub then?'

'Don't think so. Can't tell...'

'Keep the rod up,' Sodger hissed. 'Keep the line tight!'

After a few rod-bending minutes, the orange tip of the float came into view, then the rest of it, and suddenly the fish itself surfaced with a wallop and a splash.

'Bream – no, it looked like a huge roach!' Sodger exclaimed. 'But it couldn't be. Lose it and I'll kill you.'

I thought that was a bit drastic, after we'd just saved his life, but I knew what he meant.

Ken had slackened the clutch slightly and the fish screamed some line off in a rush to the far bank, but then it tired and in a few more minutes it came easily gliding into the landing net that Sodger had pushed into my hands.

It was a roach, all right. A huge roach. An amazing roach. The biggest and best roach I had ever seen. I had no idea they even grew that big.

'It's incredible!' Sodger was saying. 'Incredible! Weigh it. Quick! There's a plastic bag in my box. And a balance.'

I scrambled up and got them, then Ken carefully slid the fish into the bag and hung it on the balance while I held it up. I couldn't believe how heavy it was.

We peered at the scale while Sodger waited for the needle to settle. Then he said, 'It can't be! David...read what it says. I don't trust these dirty glasses.'

Feeling a bit like in a lesson I read what the scale said.

'Four pounds, four ounces, plus a little bit.'

'Again,' Sodger commanded.

I read it again, impressed by his excitement, but not quite understanding.

Ken had realised though.

'It's a record, isn't it – ' he began.

'Do you know what the British record is for a true roach? Do you know?' Sodger shouted.

We shook our heads.

'It's four pounds three! This fish – our fish – beats that record by a clear ounce, even allowing for the weight of the bag! Who would ever believe that a roach of that size could be found in these waters. It's the fish of a lifetime. Let's look at it. I must take a picture. Get my camera.'

Ken fetched the camera from his box and Sodger slid the fish out on to the bag so the gravel wouldn't damage it. He gently ran his finger along the big pink fin underneath it. He was counting out loud.

'Ten,' he said, after counting twice. 'Only ten rays. That means it's a true roach, not a bream hybrid. I can't believe it. I never thought I'd see a fish like it. Never in all my life!'

While we were gloating over it, full of wonder, it just lay there quietly, gills steadily pumping. I couldn't take my eyes off it; the fan-like scales were so silver and so big, all overlapping in perfect patterns, and the tail and fins were rich pink. The whole creature was fantastic.

We looked our fill, and Sodger took several photographs. He had put the camera case by it as a measure of its size. Then he said, 'That's quite long enough out of the water. Let it go now, Ken.'

Ken stared at him in amazement. He didn't move. 'But it's a record,' he said. 'Don't you know? You've got to have it witnessed – verified – or it won't count. We'll have our names in the papers and the *Angling Times* – all the fishing books –'

Then he stopped, mouth still open, as he realised what he'd said. In the silence that followed we must all have been thinking the same thought. It was incredible really. The best fish caught in England in the whole year by anybody at all – the best roach that had been caught since records began! And no-one – no-one but ourselves – could ever know about it. If they did, we'd all be in trouble – and Sodger's trouble would be the worst.

'Never mind. We'll have the pictures,' he said softly. 'I'll get you copies. Now put it back, Ken.

You never know – perhaps we'll see it again one day, when it's even bigger.'

Ken looked for a moment as if he was going to argue. But he could see there was no choice. Carefully he lifted the fabulous fish and bent down to lower it into the water.

We watched as it hovered upright in the big cage of Ken's fingers, with the water flowing gently past. It was almost perfectly still; the only movement was the steady rhythm of its gills as it recovered from the stress of being caught. But a ripple ran down its shining sides and there was a flicker from its broad tail. It tilted downwards, free of Ken's light hold. Then it surged fiercely away and was lost to sight in a second.

It was good that it was strong and free, but I was really sad to see it go.

'As a matter of interest,' Sodger was saying – not shivering at all now – 'what were you going to do, exactly, about absence notes, if you don't object to the question?'

'We hadn't really thought it out,' I said, feeling quite confident in talking to him now.

'We might have said that our Mums had rung the Secretary,' Ken said.

'I'd have checked. I always check.' He paused, as if he was thinking. Then he went on. 'This time, however, I shall certainly forget – but only this time!' He sounded like his old self now. 'Don't do it again though. It's not wise. Have you got that?'

We both nodded vigorously. We meant it, too. Once was enough! I had half a mind to ask what his excuse was, but I thought better of it.

He was moving about uncomfortably, picking up his tackle. The water in his waders sloshed and gurgled and he was giving off a damp and earthy smell.

'Now I've got to pack up and smuggle myself home before I freeze to death,' he said. 'It's been quite an experience, skiving has. I don't think I'll do it again either. Get on with your fishing you two, but take care. You've seen what can happen! And thanks. You deserve medals.'

We stood there awkwardly for a minute, as he peeled off his waders and poured a river of water out of each. He was obviously managing all right, so we climbed back up the bank, ready to go.

'See you tomorrow, sir,' I said, and we made our way, slowly this time, back to our abandoned rods.

We didn't have too much to say as I tackled up again to search for chub, and Ken went on with sprinkling maggots and trotting for those sparkling dace.

I caught two more chub, both over two

pounds, and really enjoyed the rest of the day. It hadn't been bad. After all, we did hold the British record for roach (unofficial), plus we had the blessing of Sodger himself for a day on the river.

And I bet you can guess where we'd be fishing in June, when the new season began.

TRAPPED

Last lesson Friday afternoon is a killer. We have Science and it's always bookwork, not practicals – drawings and notes, then go on to the next page and do some more. It's probably all the teachers can cope with by the end of the week, but it's boring. And Jenks likes a quiet lab. Extra boring.

But at least there's a bit of relief sometimes, like a note sliding over the acid burns on the bench.

'Early start tomorrow!' Ken's scribble.

I write, 'How early?' and shove it back.

It returns saying, 'Very early!!'

'How early is very?'

'Seriously!!!'

'How seriously?' I write anxiously.

Ken pulls a horrible face at me, behind his science book. His reply reads, 'Fatal to a lazy slob like you. Before it's light!!!'

With a crashing jangle the bell goes. Jenks' voice is drowned in the shutting of books, packing of bags, scraping of stools. There's a racket outside from the kids who are racing to get the back seats on the buses.

Me and Ken are cool. Take our time. Walk down the stairs planning tomorrow's fishing like we do most breaks and bus rides home.

'Did you mean that?' I asked, knowing he did.

'Yep. Let's beat the sun to it. Get a really early start. The river should fish well at dawn, full of massive eels and chub, all on the feed. There's a record roach too, don't forget. It might be too hot later.'

'I'm not very good at early starts,' I said. 'What sort of time are we talking about?'

'About five.' Ignoring my rude reaction, he went on, 'The forecast is for a perfect June day with mist at the start.'

'Probably pee-down,' I said.

'No it won't. Are you on?'

'You might have to wake me up,' I warned him. 'Bung little stones at the window if I don't hear the alarm. When I sleep, I die!'

'I'll chuck a brick through if you aren't ready,' Ken said.

In fact, I didn't really mind. To be out in the fields and by the water, with everyone else still asleep, sounded like a good idea. The close season had been hard to bear and the fishing should be great.

'OK,' I agreed. 'I'll get everything ready tonight, food and all, then just fall out of bed and go. I'll bring my torch.'

'You won't need that,' he said, 'unless we stay 'til dark.'

Planning the day saw us onto the bus and off the bus and up to the crossroads where we split. Mum and Dad go out on a Friday evening so later on I had the place to myself. I sorted out my tackle and tied a few hook lengths, getting everything ready.

When all was prepared, including a heap of corned beef and banana sandwiches, I watched the second part of an old film. It's the one where a submarine gets miniaturised. They send it into a man's body, with doctors, to destroy a blood clot inside his brain.

It's a rubbish film, but there's a couple of good bits where they have to steer through his arteries and valves, and white corpuscles come swimming up like monsters to attack them.

Even a stupid film like that can be a bit disturbing if you're alone in the house, and I wasn't sorry when Mum and Dad came back. I went to bed then. I warned them about my alarm going off early.

'Well, hit it quick,' Dad said. 'And bring us back some mackerel.'

Mum said, 'Don't fall in. You are going with Ken, aren't you?'

'Would I get up at that time by choice?' I asked her. 'Night all.'

I set the alarm for quarter to five, put my clothes ready and settled into bed. Of course, I couldn't get to sleep. It's never easy to relax before fishing.

I tried planning how I was going to set up my tackle tomorrow but then I found I was dwelling on the film and the journey down the arteries. That turned into a kind of scary dream, but someone going by in the street called out and I jumped awake, thinking it was Ken and I'd overslept.

The clock's luminous hands showed it was still only half past eleven so I bashed the pillow and settled again, convinced that I was going to stay awake all night.

But I must have dropped off at last, because when a new noise came it felt as if I was being dragged up out of a deep black hole. I tried to ignore it, but it came again – a fierce shower of taps and then a slither. And again. I thought, stones! On my window! Suddenly I was wide awake.

Grabbing the clock I held it in front of my eyes. Five o'clock! The alarm button was pushed in. I must have switched it off without even waking up.

I crawled down the bed and peered out. It was half-dark and there was a white mist. Ken was just a smudge down on the grass. I could see a blurred red light from where his bike must be. I waved and started dragging my clothes on. It was a good thing I'd set everything up the night before.

I felt dreadful – dry mouth, sweaty, horrible – but at least I'd had some sleep.

Ken moaned at me for not being ready, but he got over it as we neared the river. It all felt strange at this hour. There was a hint of greeny-yellow light coming across the sky, but around us was a sort of grey lake of cool mist.

We left our bikes by the fence and set off across the dewy grass. In the field it was amazingly quiet and lonely. When a dark shape lurched across our path it made us jump, but it was only a cow. We steered round a steaming cow-pat, feet breaking the silver cobwebs in the grass. Then the soft gurgle of running water told us we were nearly at the river. The old feeling of being desperate to start fishing was just speeding our steps, when another sound stopped us dead.

It was a thudding, trampling noise, followed by a bellow. Anxiously we glanced at each other. Was there a bull in the field?

A few cautious paces revealed the odd sight of a cow – looking huge in the mist – tilted up at an odd angle, and heaving backwards and forwards. It was snorting as it struggled, and as we went carefully closer we could see that it was trying to escape from some sort of pit.

It was so frightened by us appearing out of the mist that it made an even more desperate lunge and lurched up over the crumbly edge. Then it bellowed again and thundered off out of sight.

'That's weird,' Ken said. 'I've never seen that hole. Ought to be fenced off.'

We went closer, to have a look. It was more than just a hole. There seemed to have been a cave-in. The cow had only been on the edge of the down-slope, but a really big opening showed at the bottom – big enough to go in, if you bent down a bit.

'Funny place for a pot-hole,' I said. I took out my torch and shone it down over the crumpled turf of the slope and into the opening. A couple of worms wriggled out of sight as the light hit them. The beam picked out a sort of rocky arch and a tunnel leading away down under it.

Ken said, 'It must have just happened. Dump

your stuff and let's have a look. We've got all day.'

We put our tackle on the wet grass and stepped carefully down onto the collapsed turf. I had to go in front because I had the torch. The ground sank under my weight and I hoped it wasn't going to suck us in, but then there was the hardness of rock underfoot. We stooped under the stony arch and, very cautiously, edged down the steep slope.

I paused, not too happy about the way it was dropping deeper underground, but Ken whispered, 'It looks solid enough; push on a bit.'

We were in a kind of tunnel which was about head height but not quite wide enough to walk side by side. I knew it wasn't clever to keep going, but it was strange and exciting and hard to stop.

Then something ahead of us picked up the torchlight and shone against the dark. 'Watch it!' I said. 'Water.'

Very, very carefully we felt our way on down towards the brightness. When I stopped Ken was right on my shoulder.

'Wow!' he said. 'Magic!'

We were standing on a ledge, just above a narrow strip of clear water. It looked about a metre deep, though you couldn't be sure in the torch light. It was unrippled, still, and as clear as glass. The passage levelled out to run on beside it, curving round to our left and out of sight.

'Go on,' Ken urged. 'A bit further. Let's just see what's round the bend.'

'You're round the bend,' I muttered, but I went on, getting more and more jumpy and searching the ground ahead for sudden drops.

Now that the turn was cutting out all light from above, the torch was quite effective, which gave me more confidence. But then we came to a place where the roof began to dip. I wanted to stop at that point, but Ken was nudging along behind so I resisted the urge and bent forward to go on a few more steps.

It was really low for Ken and after a minute or two, to my relief, he said, 'We'd better not go much further. Just a bit more, then let's go back. We'll have to report this to someone. It's brilliant.'

Bent nearly double now, I shuffled on. Suddenly though, everything felt different. I had a feeling of space. I raised my hand and found there was nothing above my head. Carefully I stood up straight and shone the torch in a big circle. There was a muffled cry from behind, when Ken tried to stand up too, before he was out in the open.

'Serves you right!' I thought, ignoring his moans. I strained to see. The space was too great for the torch to cope with. Ghostly walls on each side showed that we were in a cavern – it felt as big as a church – and the water spread into a broad lake that shone brightly close in, then became faint and misty as it lay beyond the light.

It was as flat as a mirror. You could see the smooth stone bottom through the water at our feet, but then it ran deep and bluey-green until lost in darkness.

'D'you reckon there's fish?' Ken started to say. He stopped when his voice echoed around us, then he said 'Fish!' loudly, so that the air about our ears hissed with the fading echoes...'fish...ish...ish...' until utter silence returned.

I didn't like it, even though the place was amazing. There was too much darkness beyond the torchlight – too much silence – and I could feel the weight of the land above, pressing down on us. It seemed like it was a long way back to the real world.

He called out again – my name this time – and 'Dave' bounced round and round in the shadows so that I shushed him, afraid that the noise could bring the roof down.

Ken answered his own question, speaking softly now.

'I reckon there wouldn't be, not ordinary fish. But there's something living in all water – ' He broke off because I grabbed his arm.

I was shining the torch out across the lake, trying to see how far it stretched, and I'd suddenly become aware of a change, a movement of some kind. It was difficult to focus with nothing to fix my eyes on. Then I realised that what I could see was a ripple on the water, rolling gently and evenly towards us.

That's not much when you tell it, but it had been so fantastically still before...stiller than any water I had ever seen in my life. And now there was a ripple, coming out of the darkness and cruising silently towards where we stood on the ledge.

We watched, fascinated, as it advanced, growing clearer and brighter all the time. At last it washed gently against the rocks below our feet and faded away down the tunnel.

While we were still staring at the inch or two of darker rock wetted by the rise in the water, another ripple was already ghosting its way out of the shadows. When I took it in, seeing that it was a little higher than the first, a real shudder went through me. This one even made a sinister whispery sound as it swirled past us.

'It's weird,' I said. 'What's doing it?'

Ken said, 'Perhaps there's another opening. Perhaps something fell in.'

Nervously I scanned the torch around us. All I could see was pale rock, and water stretching into darkness. The waves had come out of a blackness that swallowed our little light.

Then another wave came seething out of the murk. The silent, steady, approach felt definitely threatening. This one was several inches high and actually splashed as it struck the ledge. Within moments another followed it and soon another. As they reached us, they lapped and slopped against the rocks, louder and louder.

'There's something out there!' I said. 'Come on, this is mad – '

But it was almost too late. At the far limit of the torchlight a change was taking place. There was a difference in the quality of the blackness. It was like a smudge, and vague so that I blinked to clear my eyes. But the smudge stayed – became more solid. As the biggest wave yet washed right up to the lip of our ledge, forcing us to back away from it, out in the shadows across the lake, something was moving. Something very big.

Even then we could still have run, but we didn't. It was like being hypnotised. We stared into the murky distance, straining our eyes to penetrate the confusing shadows and half-light created by the torch.

Now there was no doubt. Out in the furthest reaches of the water, a huge pale form was taking shape. It loomed tall, rising up against the darkness like a plume of smoke. As it stirred, ragged waves lapped and splashed around our feet.

Paralysed by fear, we stared as it became more and more horribly clear – slowly gliding closer – drawn by the echoes of our voices and the light. Not believing what I was seeing, I made out a neck and a long oval head, weaving from side to side as if searching.

The head was high, arching above us, and the thick neck merged into the mass of a body just above the water-line. I saw a glint of eyes and a dripping gap of a mouth, which opened and closed as the head rotated. And all the time it was gliding nearer.

Cold sweat was trickling down my back, and my heart pounded in my chest. At last the bit of brain I had left did its job. With the stab of a finger I snapped off the torch. It was no use though. In a moment my eyes adjusted and what they saw was ghastly.

In the absolute dark the creature glowed with a bluish light. Swaying above us now was its flattened head, as big as a mattress, with small eyes and a wide thin mouth, opening soundlessly and daggered with teeth. I glimpsed more of the body, snake-like, writhing beneath the seething surface of the water.

At that appalling moment, Ken yelled, 'Run!'

It jerked me out of the trance of terror that was gripping me. I flashed the torch on and turned in a wild panic, crashing into Ken. My foot slipped over the edge and cold water drenched my leg. I felt him grab my arm and drag me up in front of him. Then began a crazy race.

I scrambled and staggered back the way we had come, grazing my head half a dozen times on the roof, but feeling nothing in the panic and stumbling on. Then I hit a lump so hard that I saw stars; the torch flew out of my hand and splashed into the water. Too dazed to do anything, I saw the little light sink, fade to a pinpoint, and then vanish. The blackness was absolute.

Crouching, feeling sick, I clutched my head, unable to go any further and blocking Ken's way. He stopped up against me, heaving and panting, and there we stayed, afraid to move, listening, listening. All we could hear was the thumping of our hearts and the rasp of our breathing. I strained my eyes, as the stars cleared, seeking a trace of the blue glow that would mean we were being followed. Only the blackness filled them.

But in that silence, while we crouched tight together, terrified of falling into the invisible water, I heard noises.

They began with a sharp tap. Then there was a rattle and another tap followed by a positive clatter and a slithering noise. I reached to grip Ken's arm, but couldn't find it. He didn't seem to be there any more. Goosefleshed, peering into the dark, I opened my eyes so wide it hurt.

With fresh shudders going down my spine I made out something in the blackness in front of me. Not the nightmare creature, but a pale grey square. Then the clatter came again.

Sweating, afraid to make a sound, I forced my tensed-up body to crawl towards the faint light. I moved one hand forward, then the other, terrified of toppling into the water. But I was pushing through a confusing softness where there should be rock, and it was too warm to be water. Then my fingers touched hanging cloth, which parted.

I reached further and felt cold glass against my palm. Staring, I looked out into a misty half-light. There was a fuzzy red glow in the mist where a bike leaned against a fence. The tall shape of Ken was visible, standing under the window, with his arm back ready to lob another handful of gravel up.

When he saw me, he dropped the stones and pointed fiercely at his watch. then he shook his fist.

Totally muddled, I waved back and slid cautiously off the bed, still afraid of falling into water. I fumbled for the switch and put it on. It was good to be dazzled by bright light. Then I checked the clock. Quarter past five and the alarm switched off. I must have done it in my sleep.

I felt dreadful – dry mouth as if it had been

open all night, sweaty and gritty-eyed – still not sure what was dream and what was reality.

When I stumbled out with my gear, ten minutes later, Ken wasn't well-pleased.

'I knew you wouldn't be ready,' he moaned, straddling his bike. 'Get a move on. We're wasting fishing time. It's a great morning...I'm after a monster today...'

I didn't say a word.

BAITED

Part One

'I'm sick of fishing!' Ken said.

Not half as sick as I was.

It was raining. The field was slippery and awkward to walk back across. Our fishing gear was mucky and weighed a tonne. I'd spent a fortune on bait and hooks and I'd lost three floats. I was cold.

None of that mattered of course, it was just normal. But I hadn't caught any fish. Nor had Ken. Six hours of uncomfortable fishing on a windy February day and not even a bite. Even worse, it had been the same the week before. And the week before that.

Three times in a row we had blanked. It was never that bad before. Blame the rain that kept coming down. Blame the temperature that kept going up and down. Blame –

'I blame the fish,' Ken said. 'They won't feed – not even the gudgeon. What's up with them?'

'Nothing gets them going,' I agreed. 'Maggots, casters, bread, sweetcorn, worm, cheese, luncheon meat – you name it, we've tried it. What more can we do!'

'What we want,' Ken said thoughtfully, 'is a bait they can't refuse.'

'A lump of Semtex?' I suggested.

'No,' he said. 'I mean it. I've always had the idea that there must be something...something no-one's ever tried. Something that fish would go crazy over, every time...'

'There's loads of bait additives in the House of Angling,' I said. 'Raspberry, banana, worm essence.'

'Yes, but if they really worked we'd know,' he interrupted. 'My uncle used to say those things only catch anglers. But there ought to be something...Something new...'

'OK, what?'

'Dunno. How about doing some experiments next weekend?'

'What do you mean – different flavours?'

'Yes, and colours and textures and smells – way-out stuff. Everything.'

I said, 'We'll need a way of testing them. You can't really find out just by putting them in the river.'

'I've thought about that,' Ken said. 'We'll try them on Arry.' He was sounding keen now. Arry's the only goldfish left in Dad's pond, the rest all vanished. Arry never takes any food we put in, so if he goes for a bait, it must be a winner.'

We reached our bikes and got on them, sticky with wet and mud, and rode home. I was feeling quite cheerful. Next weekend would be devoted to scientific experiment. Anything would be better than fishing!

All through the week I kept my eyes open for possible samples. Mum's cupboards lost a lot of little spoonfuls, all bagged in separate twists of clingfilm, identified by freezer labels. I sacrificed some Mars Bar and smashed up a couple of Extra-strong mints. I used bits from the garden – berries and seed pods – and even crushed up some leaves from the evergreen, until I realised it might be poisonous. There was onion and garlic in the store and cough medicine in the bathroom. We kept lists and compared them in school during the week to make sure we hadn't duplicated. Ken had big hopes for the spices – his Mum was into Indian cooking –

and he had some bits of weird vegetables and fruit too.

When Saturday came we set our specimens out in Ken's Dad's shed. We went about it scientifically. First we spread clean newspaper on the bench, then we laid out the forty-six different ingredients we'd selected, making sure the labels were on them.

Bread paste was going to be the base, and Ken had dreamed up a device to test out four baits at once.

It was a wire coathanger, with four lengths of fishing line hanging from the bar. At the bottom of each line he had nipped on a number 6 shot to squeeze the bait round, rather than risk, as he said, getting 'an 'ook into Arry.'

So that we wouldn't get muddled, we numbered all the flavours. Number one was custard powder and number forty-six was Barbecue Relish. The idea was to make up four at a time, pinch them onto the four shots in number order, and lower them in Ken's little garden pond for Arry to inspect.

At this time Arry was about eight inches long, and still growing. He never took fishfood – perhaps having the pond all to himself, apart from the newts and frogs, meant there was enough natural food to keep him going. But for a fish he was quite friendly, and he'd come and have a look at you when you went near, before drifting off on his own business.

So we made four pellets of bread paste. Into one I mixed some yellow custard powder and into another I squeezed some mustard. Ken prepared three and four with a drop of his Dad's whisky and some chilli powder. We kept them in number order when we squeezed them on the weights, then Ken leaned over the pond and gently lowered the hanger until all four baits had broken the surface and were dangling a few inches under.

'Come on Arry,' he whispered. 'Din-dins.'

Out came Arry, gliding fat and gold from under some rotten lily leaves. He kind of glanced up at us, then went for a quiet tour round the baits. He gave the mustard one a little knock with his nose, sending it swinging, and he flicked his tail at the whiskey. Then he did a second run past them, blew a bubble and let himself drift gently down until we could hardly see him. And there he stopped.

'OK Arry, 'ang about and we'll be back,' Ken promised.

Back to the shed we went, prepared four more temptations and tried again. But neither curry, nor blue cheese dressing, nor garlic, nor Mars Bar attracted Arry at all.

We still didn't get despondent. It took about eight sets of samples before a sense of hopelessness set in.

It wasn't Arry's fault. He really co-operated.

With each new set he helpfully did his patrol. You could tell that he wanted to like them – but he just couldn't. The Stir-Fry Black Bean Sauce gave us a flicker of hope when he had a second sniff, but it came to nothing.

It was quite clear, when we reached the eleventh set – with only two left to try – that it wasn't going to be easy to find what anglers must have been seeking for hundreds of years. I more or less gave up hope and went back towards the shed to finish reading a football report that had caught my eye in the paper on the bench.

Ken's shout – 'Dave! Dave!' – brought me running back to the pond.

He was holding up the hanger, and from it dangled a line with a lump of paste on – and a line with only a number six shot! He looked staggered.

It fell off,' I said, hoping it hadn't.

'No!' he yelled. 'Arry ate it! He had a couple of sniffs, a suck, and it was gone!'

'Which was it?' I asked, getting keen now. 'Which bait?'

Don't know. Didn't bother to check,' he confessed.

'Doesn't matter,' I said. 'There's only two it can be.'

We rushed back in and made up two more blobs with the scrapings of the last two flavours –

crushed peanuts, and Barbecue Relish. Then we went back to Arry.

Very slowly, with a shaky hand, Ken lowered the baits until they hovered above the water, then dimpled its surface, then broke through and swayed slightly just beneath it.

We didn't have to wait. There was a stir in the murky depths, a quick flash of gold, a splash, and one of the baits was snatched so fast that Ken jerked his arm up in surprise. If the bait hadn't come off, Arry would have been shot up into the air like a rocket.

'Which one?' I shouted.

It was the second line that was empty.

'We've got it!' Ken yelled. 'The perfect bait. Barbeque Relish!'

H'm. Barbeque Relish. The perfect bait. Might be. Somehow I couldn't see it. It was too easy.

'Try again,' I suggested. 'If it happens three times it must mean something.'

Of course, we'd run out of Relish – I'd only brought a smear. Into Ken's house we went. Hustled his Mum into hunting out half a jar of the stuff, and then back into the laboratory. Then to the pond.

Total failure! Arry came up keenly, opened his mouth around the bait, paused, fins fanning gently, then went into reverse, looked up at us with disappointment clear in his body language, and sank miserably back into the green darkness.

Ken tried hard to persuade him. He almost fell in himself, leaning over to lower the bait right onto where he thought Arry's nose must be. But Arry stayed put. Not interested.

'Perhaps he's full up,' I said.

'Never. It's something else. I can't think...we must have done something different. He was mad on it before. There must be a reason!'

At that moment his Mum came out to see how things were going.

'Do I get my Relish back?' she asked, 'or do you two have to go to Sainsbury's for some more?'

I looked at the jar that I was still holding. 'That's it!' I yelled. 'Tesco!'

'Don't you mean "Eureka"?' she asked.

'No,' I said. 'It's the wrong stuff. Ours is Tesco's.'

'Different mixture!' Ken shouted, but I didn't answer because by then I was on my way to my bike and another raid on Mum's cupboard.

Well, it worked. It worked fantastically. Tesco's Relish drove Arry wild. He'd have taken it until he burst, if we'd given him the chance. He loved it so much that he even came out of the water to meet it by the time we got to the fifth little pink pellet.

Ken and I sat back on our heels and shook hands.

'Pity we can't go tomorrow,' I said. 'But roll on next Saturday.'

Ken agreed. 'It's going to be a long week,' he said.

Suddenly we weren't fed up with fishing after all.

Part 2

But it was a terrible week. It rained nearly all day, every day. We were soaked waiting for the bus in the mornings and soaked going out of school for it in the afternoons. Games on the field were cancelled because we might have drowned. The seagulls took over the pitches even though we are miles from the sea.

When it got to Friday, the clouds began to break at last, but we knew just how bad the river would be – up to the top of the banks, if not over them, full of branches and weed, and unfishable.

Friday lunch-time, as we ate our sandwiches in the school canteen, we tried to convince ourselves that it would still be OK, but we knew we'd had it. Until Ken had the brain wave.

'Canal!' he said. 'That's what we need – some canal fishing. No flow, no flood – it's all done by locks and sluice gates. We did it in Geography last year, remember?'

'Where's the nearest?' I asked doubtfully. 'We'd have to get there.'

'My Dad'll know. They go walking along canals sometimes. I'll find out tonight and ring you.'

I wasn't very hopeful. Everything was so soggy, and the fields – seen from the top of the school bus – had lakes in them.

But at half past six the phone rang and it was Ken with good news.

'Parents have their uses,' he said. 'They're glad of an excuse for a day's walking. Must be mad! My Dad rang a bloke at work who fishes and he said just past Devizes is good. A village called Seend. So they'll drop us there, walk all day and pick us up at the end. They've got their maps and boots out already.'

'Brilliant!' I said. 'I'll make up a load of Magic Bait. Do we need any other stuff, d'you reckon?'

'Not if it's as good as we think it is. But we can stop off at the House of Angling on the way. Godfrey'll tell us what's best for the canal. Next week we might be selling him our secret formula!'

'I'm really RELISHING the thought of tomorrow,' I said. 'Get it?'

'No,' Ken said. 'Too clever for me. Pick you up tomorrow then. About half-eight.'

They parked the car by a bridge, just below the village, and walked along the canal with us to a spot where we decided to set up. Then they said goodbye and vanished into the sunrise with their boots and rucksacks and map case.

The weather had completely changed, though the air still had a haze of moisture in it. Even that might clear, as the sun went on rising. The canal looked nice. The lock gates along to our right had great timbers to open them with, painted bright white, with black ends, and there was a little bridge humped over the canal, where they'd left the car.

We settled down on the narrow strip of grass that lies between the towpath and the canal. Behind us was a low hedge, and in front, across the water,

was the garden of a pub, with wooden benches and tables for summer evenings.

It was quiet and I felt very content as we set up our float rods. I took out the big ball of Magic Bait that I'd prepared. It was a stiff bread paste made with white bread, with a good dollop of Barbecue Relish well mixed into it so that it was an even, rich pink colour.

'Hang on to that for a bit,' Ken said.

'What d'you mean?'

'Let's try the ordinary stuff first. It'll give us a better idea of how good it is.'

We'd spent the whole week thinking and dreaming about our discovery, but funnily enough it didn't seem quite so important now. I just wanted to fish. So I agreed with Ken's idea and set up with a tiny float and a size 22 hook.

Godfrey, in the fishing shop, had advised starting with pinkies and then moving on to maggots if the bigger fish came on the feed. I'd never seen pinkies before, but it sounded like good advice. Pinkies are a really small maggot, almost too small to handle – and they're bright pink just like our Magic Bait.

It was quite easy to set up the float so that only its tip showed above the flat surface of the canal. And it was really comfortable at the edge of the water, with the firm towpath behind. All we needed now was some fish.

I sat watching the float and enjoying the watery sound from the mossy lock gates, where spray fountained out through a gap at the side to trickle down the stone wall. It was a picture-postcard scene, with the old pub, and the village rising up above the bridge on its low hill.

When my float twitched under I struck lightly and easily reeled in a little roach, with dazzling silver scales and bright pink fins. It had a softer feel to it than the tougher river fish that I was used to.

At almost the same moment, Ken was landing a small bream. It was very satisfactory – gentler than the river, but good fishing. And we still had the Magic Bait to try.

After a while we'd both caught nine or ten small roach and bream, and we changed up to proper maggots and size eighteen hooks. That slowed things down a bit, though I did land a bream that was about half a pound, and Ken lost a really big perch, just over the net.

We were using barbless hooks, which is great when you're catching small fish, but you do lose a few fish if you don't keep the line tight. All the same, you still probably catch more fish with them, because you don't waste so much time trying to unhook them from your trousers or the back of your neck.

We went on catching, quite steadily – smallish fish, but nice ones: roach, rudd, bream, perch and – naturally – a few gudgeon. After the fishless times we'd been having, it was great. In fact it was so enjoyable that I had almost forgotten about the experiment.

But when we made ourselves stop for a sandwich, Ken said, 'Right, we know what maggots and pinkies can do. Now let's try the other.'

I agreed – if it didn't work we could always go back to the maggots – and took off the small hook and the light trace. I tied a size 14 hook straight to the three pound line and squeezed a small pellet of the prepared paste on to it, with the tip of the hook just showing.

'If we're right,' I said, 'they'll go mad for it, so we might as well take the big ones.'

Came the moment for the first cast. I hung on until Ken was ready too, then out went our floats and we waited, tense, for the instant take.

Which didn't come.

The roach and the rudd and the bream and the perch that we'd been catching all morning simply ignored our special-can't-fail Barbecue Relish Magic Bait. Not even a gudgeon showed an interest. The floats just sat there, unmoving.

'I don't believe this,' Ken said, after about ten

minutes. 'Arry loved it and we know the canal's full of fish. Perhaps the hooks are too big.'

After another ten minutes with no action at all, he started to reel in ready to tackle back down to something lighter.

'Perhaps we've caught so many that we've spooked them,' I suggested.

With that in mind, I thought I'd try a bit deeper, so I reeled in too and raised the float to get the bait close to the bottom. I re-cast – nearly too far because it went right under the far bank – and found that I'd set it too deep because the float was lolling around on the surface, hardly cocked at all.

It didn't matter though, because it wasn't there for more than a moment. Within seconds something ripped it away out of sight.

I called to Ken as my rod arched and line shrieked off in the direction of the bridge. It brought me to my feet, heart thumping.

What followed was a real fight, specially after all the small fish we'd been catching, but I didn't intend to lose this one. Ken joined me, landing net ready, and after about five minutes of good action the float came back up into view, an orange stick on the surface. A metre or so beyond it there was something else...something big and kicking... something that was bright orange too!

Ken gave a great crow of laughter and I nearly

forgot to keep the tension on the line.

Still thrashing angrily, but not running, a huge goldfish came steadily nearer and nearer until Ken, arm shaking from the laughing, was able to lift it cleanly out and draw it in over the bank.

While it lay there in the landing net I nicked the hook free and stared at the great heaving side – partly orange and splashed with white – and the broad, pale gold tail. I hadn't come to catch goldfish but it was certainly a superb specimen.

Ken had finally stopped laughing and was inspecting it closely.

'I don't think it is a goldfish,' he said. 'I reckon it's a koi carp. They cost a bomb if you buy them for ponds. Wonder where it came from.'

'You'd better take it home for Arry,' I said. 'They might fancy each other.'

'It'd eat Arry,' Ken said. 'But it's an idea, if we could get it home alive.'

We put it in my keepnet where it must have caused a bit of a sensation amongst the humble roach and bream. Then I adjusted the float slightly and cast out again with a fresh ball of Magic Bait on the hook. I hoped that the big catch hadn't scared off all the proper fish.

The float poised more neatly now and I watched it for all of a minute before down it went again. The swirl, just under the surface, showed how fast the fish had seized it.

But it was a repeat of last time except this time it took longer because the fish was even bigger. This one was almost white, with flaming orange spots across its back and tail. We weighed it before sliding it into the keepnet. It was three and a half pounds of fine, fat fish.

Ken said, 'It works. The bait does work, but –'

'Yes,' I said. 'It works, but does it only work on goldfish...or whatever they are? Could that be?'

'Don't know,' Ken said. 'But I'll put a bigger hook on and join you.'

It was quite warm and sunny now, specially for February. Glimpsing a movement across the water I even saw that a bloke was settling down with his newspaper and a pint on one of the garden seats outside the pub.

It made me thirsty, so I put off making the next cast until I'd had a swig of fruit juice and a chocolate biscuit. Then I baited up again and Ken and I both cast, so that our floats bobbed up and settled, quite close to each other.

In less than three minutes I was into another fish. It ran towards the bridge, which was just as well because as I jumped to my feet I heard Ken exclaim as his float dived.

It was all concentration then, especially when the fish came close in. We had to keep side-strain on, to avoid tangling our lines. In the end we landed them almost simultaneously.

There they were, side by side on the grass: two fat white and orange monsters – mine splodged with dark brown as well – great to feel on the line, but still not really what we had come for.

As I raised mine up, to slip the hook out of its wide, round mouth, I heard a smash of glass, a shout and pounding footsteps. I glanced across the water to see pages of a newspaper fluttering into the canal and a running figure leaving the pub garden. Weird!

We spent a few moments admiring the big fish and looking at their separate markings, then put them back into the water in our nets.

'I'm sure it's the bait,' Ken said. 'But I don't get why there are fish like this in here.'

'Perhaps there *are* koi carp in canals,' I suggested.

'Never! We'd know. And you wouldn't have to pay so much for them in the water-garden centres.'

'We can open our own,' I said, 'after this. But perhaps you're wrong. Perhaps there always have been fish like this about, but people never used bread paste and Tesco's Barbecue Relish, so no-one knew.'

'Believe that and you'll believe anything,'

Ken said. 'No. We've boobed. Arry was the wrong sort of fish to try it on. It's a dead selective bait – it just attracts goldfish and their cousins. Still, these could be worth a fortune – '

He stopped short then because the sound of running feet drew our attention to the fact that the bloke from the pub garden had crossed the bridge, slid down the slope onto the tow path and was thundering towards us.

I felt a bit anxious. Had we done something wrong? Perhaps you weren't supposed to fish there. Because of the koi carp.

'Here's trouble,' I muttered, sweating rather.

Before he got to us the bloke shouted something. And then again. He was gasping but I made out the words.

'My fish!' he cried. 'My fish!'

Then he was at my shoulder, coughing and wheezing so much that I thought he was going to drop dead on the spot.

At last he got over it and straightened up. Tears were rolling down his red cheeks.

'You're catching my fish!' he gasped. 'My fish – ' and then he was off into another coughing fit.

I thought, Oh hell. We shouldn't be here. It's private or a sort of nature reserve or something.

I began to say, 'The sign says Devizes Angling

Club...' but he was bending over my keepnet by now, peering down into the green water.

'Let me see them,' he was begging. 'Oh please let me see them!'

I looked at Ken, who shrugged then came over to stand by me. We were both thinking that he must be a bit of a nutter – probably harmless, but there wasn't anyone else about. It was more embarrassing than alarming.

Anyway, to keep him happy, I half lifted my keepnet so that the fish were visible but still well in the water. In amongst the little roach and bream, the three big mottled carp were hovering like visiting gods.

'It's Roger!' the man exclaimed. 'It is – it's Roger Smart. I never thought I'd see him again. And there – look – ' I had to grab his arm because he was nearly in the net with them by now, but he didn't stop babbling. 'It's Stan – Stan Harland. And Peter Noble. How ever did you find them?'

He was looking at me now as if I'd won him the lottery or something. I thought, he's definitely mad.

Then he was trying to lift Ken's net, so Ken went to help – or make sure he didn't empty the net back into the canal. When Ken showed him the contents he actually stood there clapping, as if Ken had just scored a goal.

'Oh yes, oh yes!' he shouted. 'Peter Downsborough! The keeper himself. It's too good to be believed...'

Then he flopped down onto my tackle box, took out a handkerchief and started mopping his forehead and eyes. He kept making little excited grunts and looking from one net to the other as if to make sure they were real.

Eventually he got his breath back and began to calm down. He saw us standing there, looking at him doubtfully, and introduced himself.

'Sorry about all that,' he said. 'Must have made you jump a bit. I'm Andrew West. Who are you?'

We told him and he went on. 'Right then Ken...and Dave. You've just done something brilliant...'

Well, he wasn't really a nutter at all. Not quite. He told us how, back in September, there had been a freak rain storm – a cloudburst – and his garden, up beyond the bridge, had flooded. Half his precious collection of koi carp had taken the opportunity to swim out of their luxurious pond and go off into the big wide world of the canal. He hadn't expected ever to see them again.

'How many did you lose, exactly?' Ken asked.

'Seven...seven of the best. Over half the team.'

'Uh...team?' Ken asked.

'I had twelve. Eleven players and one sub. They all had names, you see. You remember when Swindon beat Arsenal in the League Cup Final at Wembley – no of course you don't – '

'I've heard of it,' I said. My Dad went, and he's still got the programme. Didn't a player called Don Rogers score two goals?'

'That's right! That's right! Both in extra time. What a game! Anyway, I named the fish after the team. Now then, you've got four in the net. There's three more out there somewhere – we've got to get them!' He realised he was shouting and dropped to a whisper, as if he was afraid of scaring the fish. 'You're not stopping are you. Please don't stop!'

He didn't leave us a lot a lot of choice, but we were getting almost as keen as he was, so we baited up and cast again. We were both standing, ready for action, while Andrew sat on my box between us. He was quiet now, staring at our floats as tensely as we were.

When Ken was suddenly back into the action, Andrew was there with the landing net, and I had to tell him what to do, how to keep it still and wait. He found that really hard – he wanted to jump in and grab the fish himself – but he more or less managed and Ken got the fish into the net as quickly as he safely could.

It was a very long specimen that came out, darkly marked in a pattern like a big jigsaw.

'Rod Thomas!' shouted Andrew. Then he dropped his voice again. 'Brilliant defender!' he whispered, and he gave the fish a little pat before letting Ken add it to his collection.

Soon after, Ken caught another. 'John Smith. Striker,' rejoiced Andrew. That left just one more.

Time passed and he began to get anxious. After a quarter of an hour he was desperate.

'It's Don Rogers himself,' he kept saying. 'Where is he? What could have happened to him?'

Rather cruelly, I thought, Ken said, 'Perhaps a pike's had him!'

'What do you mean?'

'There must be some huge pike in a stillwater like this,' Ken explained. 'I reckon they'd be attracted by big coloured fish like these.'

Andrew just laughed at him.

Ken was a bit offended. 'I meant it,' he said. 'You get really big pike in canals, much bigger than these we've been catching.'

Andrew laughed again. 'Not a chance,' he said confidently. 'No chance of that happening. Don't you worry about that.'

Ken took his eyes off his float to give him a puzzled look.

'I don't get it,' he said. 'Why not?'

'Look, my boy. That fish out there is Don Rogers. Do you think a miserable pike could be fast enough to catch a winger with the speed and swerve he's got? The best defenders in the league couldn't stop him!'

Ken didn't even try to answer that one.

I felt that things were getting a bit confusing, but before I had time to sort it out my float vanished at last, with a dramatic swirl.

'That's him! That's him!' Andrew yelled. 'He's going for goal!'

'He's going for those bushes,' Ken muttered. 'Hold him, Dave.'

I had to put some pressure on, to turn him away from the far bank, then I let him run. It would have been risky not to. He certainly had a turn of speed. When I could, I took in some line, only to hear it tear back off the reel. I slackened the clutch a bit more, so violent were the runs. This was one fish I really mustn't lose.

The bloke was going demented beside me each time the fish took off.

'He's going down the wing now,' he was shouting. 'He's round the full back, he's coming right across the park, he's in the middle, what a swerve, now he's off down the wing again, he's cutting in, he's right in front of the net...' as the fish came almost close enough to land...then, as it set off on another run across the canal...'Oh sod it, he's gone again! Can't you just drag him in? Watch it, here he comes again – '

'Go on Dave,' Ken snorted. 'Tackle him, bring him down...'

And while all this was going on around me, I was trying to play the creature sensibly, so that it didn't snap the line and probably be lost for good. It was one of the most difficult catches I'll ever make.

Still, even Don Rogers couldn't keep it up for ever, and at last a very tired player came limping in to the bench and was netted by Andrew as gently as if he'd had to play double extra time.

Once the fish was lying on the grass, little hook removed from huge mouth, its owner was quite speechless. He just crouched there, holding its tail and making baby noises.

I looked at Ken and we burst out laughing, but it wasn't aimed at Andrew. It was for sheer pleasure and relief. It really was amazing to have recaptured all seven fish.

It was strange how the little shoal had stuck together, come through the lock at some point and settled in the spot where we happened to be fishing. Perhaps people in the pub garden dropped bits of food in and it reminded them of home.

We persuaded Andrew to let us put the fish

into my keepnet, and he calmed down enough to start thinking about how he was going to transport them.

He asked us how long we were going to be there, and said he'd go off and organise something. We said we'd wait for him and promised to look after them until he came back.

We made sure the nets were pegged out fully, so the fish had room to move around, but without any chance of them making a break for freedom. I have known a big chub jump right out the end of a keepnet.

Then we went back to fishing with pinkies and maggots, and catching nice little bream and roach. It wasn't as exciting as having the big carp on the end but it seemed a lot more natural. We didn't put any into the keep nets, not to crowd the precious carp. We were having a very good time.

'Caught anything?' Ken's Dad asked, as people always do, and Ken was just trying to find an answer that would do justice to the occasion when his voice was drowned by the clatter of a motor behind us. A tractor, towing a trailer, pulled up just the other side of the hedge.

Andrew had mobilised his farmer friend and they had tied an old bath onto the trailer with water in it. He handed a plastic sack over the low hedge.

'Watch that Don Rogers,' he said. 'He'll go

past you if you're not careful.'

When we lifted Ken's net out of the water and laid it out on the grass his Mum and Dad stopped asking questions and just stared. They were lost for words. There was no time to explain. We had to work fast, lifting the big fish one at a time, slipping them into the sack and passing them to Andrew.

Once the carp were safely out, the net had to be emptied of small fish, so they could swim away and recover from the shock of being jumped on by the giants. Then we lifted out my net.

Once again the swift move took place, from keep net, to sack, to old bath. When the last one was safely transferred Andrew called, 'Don't go away. I'll be round.'

While the tractor chuntered slowly off, Ken explained what had been going on. Looking over the hedge I could see Andrew balanced on the trailer, watching over his fish and making sure they didn't slop out.

The tractor stopped just past the bridge and he came walking back towards us – not rushing like last time.

Ken introduced him to his Mum and Dad and he gave them a card with his name and address on. He said we all had to visit him and see the fish back on their own pitch. Come when we like, just give him a ring. Come for drinks. A meal. A barbeque when it's warmer. How grateful he was. How brilliant we were – and fishing must be expensive, please accept this, goodbye, must see to the lads now...five of them are girls actually... goodbye, goodbye...'

And there we were, left holding a bit of paper each. I looked at mine. A cheque for a hundred pounds. A reward.

Ken's Mum said, 'Looks like your bait worked, then.'

'Like magic,' I said. 'Just like magic.'

MATCHED

'You're kidding,' Ken said easily. 'Not even a berk like you could be that much in love.'

When I didn't answer he asked me again, with a touch of anxiety creeping in.

'You are kidding, aren't you?'

I went a bit hot and shook my head.

'It's a sick joke. You don't mean it?...You do mean it!'

'Yes,' I admitted, 'she asked – '

'And you said yes?' he shouted. 'That's the thickest thing I ever heard! How's she going to get there? What's she going to do all day? She'll scare the fish off. It'll be a waste of time...ruin everything.'

Lost for words he stopped, staring at me angrily. I didn't like seeing him upset, but what could I do?

I'd been going out with Jan ever since she was moved up into my Maths set at the beginning of Year Eleven. Until the last couple of weeks she'd helped in her Gramp's shop on a Saturday, so Ken hadn't really been affected by her, except as an excuse for making boring jokes. Now her Gramp had sold the shop and she'd lost her job. That's how she had come to surprise me as we straggled out of assembly on Friday.

'When are you going to take me fishing?' she asked. That stopped me dead, so that the others had to swirl round us, like water round a stone in the river.

I looked at her, well surprised, but she smiled – and with that smile and her dark hair and all, there was only one answer.

'Whenever,' I said. 'Tomorrow if you like.'

'OK Dave, what time?'

I'd already planned with Ken that we were going to try for barbel at Water Eaton, but I didn't see a problem. I had a little rod she could use – one of those beginners' kits. My aunt had given me it. They aren't much use, but I thought it would do for her to play with.

Now she had suggested it, I quite fancied

showing her the river and how to fish. She was a good laugh anyway, and a whole day together would be great.

We go about eight,' I said. 'Have you got wellies and all? You might get muddy.'

'I have fished before, you know,' she said. 'With my other Gramp. He was really good. Are we going on our bikes..?'

Well, Ken went quiet after I admitted my crime. When we split to go to our houses, I said, 'We'll be round about eight, OK?'

The 'we' was mean, but I risked it, and I liked the sound of it anyway. What Ken said in reply can't be printed here and I went home feeling a bit flat. We'd never had bad feelings before, not even when we'd tangled each other's lines. I half wondered if he was jealous.

At six o'clock that evening things got worse. The phone rang.

'Hi Dave,' Jan said. 'It's OK for tomorrow. But my Gramp's got to go to Bristol for the day and he says he'll drop us at Sutton Benger and pick us up on the way back in the evening. I couldn't just say no, 'cos he'd already bought us three day-tickets when he told me. It's on the River Avon. That's where my other Gramp used to to take me. I haven't been back there since he died. I didn't want to at first, but I'd really like to now. It is good there.

Would you mind?'

'No, course not,' I said, thinking, 'What the hell is Ken going to say?'

'We'll pick you up about eight,' she said, 'then Ken. See you Dave.'

'Yes, 'night,' I said, putting down the phone and dreading having to tell Ken that Jan had changed our plans for us – unless he chose to spend the day by himself, and I didn't want him to do that.

When I finally got myself round to phoning him, it wasn't as bad as I feared. He was still a bit cold, but he'd read about Sutton Benger in the local paper and I could tell he was interested in the chance of fishing there.

I got on with packing my stuff, dug a few worms and made some sandwiches (not with the worms) then went to bed, looking forward to it all.

It took about half an hour to get there. Straight down the M4, then through the village and down a long narrow road, under a railway bridge and into a little layby. Jan did the navigating.

I liked her Gramp although he didn't say much. Ken and I sat in the back and didn't say much either, but it felt like quite an adventure, going off to fish a new water, and having to work out how to fish it, once we got there.

When they opened the back of the car to take the gear out, I was surprised at the well-used rod bag that Jan had brought, but I didn't say anything. She had the rest of her stuff in a rucksack, with a stool on the side, like I did.

'I'll come and find you,' her Gramp said. 'There's no hurry, so fish as long as you like. Look after each other –'Bye.'

He reversed the car, tooted the horn and we were left alone on the quiet little road.

'The river's through that gate,' Jan said, hoisting on her rucksack and shouldering the rod bag that was nearly as long as she was.

We followed her through the gate and across the corner of a flat, ploughed field, on a well trodden path. Now I could hear an exciting roar of water, even though it wasn't visible yet.

Then we caught glimpses of the river down through bushes to our right, and a big stone house up on the far side.

The roar of water came from a wide, stepped weir, with a great concrete kind of sluice-gate at the side of it. A small waterfall sprayed down over rocks in the far corner. My eyes were held, as they always are, by the swirling, foaming water so that it was startling when a heron suddenly rose from the calmer pool in front of us with slow beats of its long wings.

Ken wasn't talking, but he was certainly looking. Besides being excited by the water, I was feeling relieved. It was working out all right.

'I love this place,' Jan said, 'but it does remind me of Gramps.' Her voice wobbled and I saw her swallow. I'd have put my arm round her if the rod-bag and rucksack weren't in the way.

'Lucky there's no-one else here, though,' she said, suddenly cheerful again. 'He'd have liked that. Come on down.'

There was a stony bank between some willows, and then we were standing on a gravelly beach. The water thundered down on our left, paused in the wide pool in front of us, then wandered off along the rushy riverbed on its journey to Bristol and the sea.

'There's plenty of room for three,' Jan said, dumping her stuff. 'Where do you two want to fish? I'll let you choose.'

I knew what Ken would say.

'Up here,' he grunted, beginning to move his gear along to the left hand corner of the beach. He was looking hungrily at the bubbling water below the weir. Barbel were on his mind.

I liked the streamy bit to the right, so I started to move that way. Chub, I was thinking. That left Jan in the middle, with the pool in front of her.

'Good,' she said happily. 'Bream, if I'm lucky. Now then, rules of the match -'

'Match?' Ken turned suddenly at the word.

'Don't you always have a match?' Jan asked, as if surprised. 'Gramps and me always had a match. It was fun. I beat him sometimes, when I was lucky.'

'What rules?' Ken asked, looking keen.

'We always had three classes,' she said. 'Who catches the biggest fish – fish of the day, we called it – who catches the most fish, and who catches the biggest number of different species. Little ones like bleak and minnows don't count.'

'What about heaviest total weight?' Ken demanded.

'We didn't do that,' Jan said. ''Cos it's a bit cruel to lift out the keepnet and weigh them all in a heap. It damages their scales. Often we just kept count and didn't use a net at all.'

'Fair enough,' he agreed. 'But we'd better use keepnets today or else Dave'll cheat like he usually does.'

Ken was obviously happy now. He always was competitive and I saw the light of battle in his eyes. He'd get his own back on me for bringing Jan. And he'd show her what real fishing was all about – that was what the look in his eyes said.

Jan came over to me for some maggots, just as I was taking my float rod out. Unfortunately, the beginners' rod that I'd brought for her, still in its bright blue plastic case, slid out too. I tried to push it out of sight under the bag but she saw it and picked it up and looked at the little two-piece rod, crappy reel and big striped float.

I went red as she examined it.

'What's this then?' she grinned.

'Is that still in there?' I blustered. 'I keep meaning to get rid of it...' I didn't dare say I'd brought it for her. 'My aunt gave me it...typical! It's no use to anyone...'

I once caught a trout on a rod like that,' Jan said.'On holiday with Gramp and Gran. 'But it was only on a fish farm, so it doesn't really count.'

I breathed again, and stuck the package back in my bag. I've never caught a trout anywhere.

She took some maggots and casters, scruffed my hair up, and went along to her stool. Out of the corner of my eye I saw her setting up a quiver-tip rod with a swim feeder. Then she arranged her stuff neatly to hand and carefully lined up two rod rests. I saw Ken glancing down with a surprised look on his face. She didn't need any help at all. It was quite disappointing.

While I was still fiddling with hooks and shot, she flicked her rod and a splash across the pool, under the little waterfall, showed where the swim feed had been set. A moment later her rod was on the rests and she was fishing.

It took me ages to get my stick float shotted

so that it just dragged the bottom, and I looked across to see Ken make his first cast, up under the full force of the weir. Luncheon meat, on a size ten hook, I reckoned he'd be using, with a bomb to hold it against the pressure.

At last I was ready too, and with a sprinkling of maggots from the catapult, and a single maggot on the size 20 hook, I made my first proper cast. The float trotted slowly out of the tail of the pool and away past the rushes. I kept a finger against the open spool, steadying the pace and keeping the line fairly tight to the float.

The water was loud as it roared down the weir, so talking was difficult. For a while we fished in friendly silence, keen to see the first fish. I quite fancied the match idea.

I fancied it even more when my float dived. It felt like a good little fish when I struck, and I was a bit disappointed when I found it was the usual wriggling gudgeon.

'What's that?' came Ken's jealous voice, as Jan called, 'Number one to Dave.'

I slipped it into the net – though I wouldn't normally keep it – and lowered the float a bit to lift the bait off the bottom. I didn't want to catch gudgeon all day. Still, I was in the lead now: best fish, biggest variety, most fish – in fact, only fish!

Not for long though. Jan gave a squeak and I

saw her lift her rod sharply. It arched over in a tight bend, switching from side to side as she steadily played a lively fish. I went to help, but she already had the landing net in the water and I just watched as a really nice bream came wallowing into it.

'Great,' she said. 'About a pound. What a start!' And she crouched to unhook it, before transferring it to her keepnet.

Wiping her hands on the piece of towel that she had lain it on, she said, 'Aren't they slimy. But they do feel good on the line!'

Ken was looking to see what was going on, then he turned back to focus on his rod. I knew how he'd be feeling. I felt the pressure myself.

Now we were fishing hard, concentrating, looking for every touch but keeping an anxious eye on each other as well. The fight was on.

It wasn't long before Jan gave an excited laugh and played in another bream – bigger than the first one.

'Well done,' I called, feeling sick, and casting again. I was wishing I'd chosen the place she was fishing. There didn't seem any fish at all where I was.

I glanced past her at Ken, to see him make a huge strike, only to find he had a gudgeon flying through the air, straight at his face. With a quiet, unkind snigger I looked back at my own float. It wasn't there!

I struck gently – experimentally – to find a real weight on the end. I began to play it steadily, with the clutch set light, and the invisible fish made a couple of runs before I was able to steer it carefully through the gap in the rushes in front of me, and net it.

'Chub,' I called. 'About a pound and a half.'

'Great, Dave,' Jan said.

Ken came down and had a quick look, but said nothing.

I was really concentrating after that, when Jan called out to me. She was pointing at Ken, up by the weir. He was on his feet, rod tip high in the air and tugging violently. I could see the effort he was making to hold the fish.

We both put our rods down and went to join him and watch the fight.

'It must be barbel,' he gasped. 'Really big. Nearly took the rod into the river.'

I'd never seen anything like it. One moment the line was cutting through the reeds to the left of the weir, the next minute it was scything through the foam in the very centre, before screaming in towards where we stood, faster than Ken could take up the slack.

It swerved, and made a run to the right, out

into the main pool, repeating the circuit several times before suddenly seeming to tire and coming almost easily towards us. We still hadn't seen it at this point.

Jan had grabbed the landing net and was holding it in the water, waiting for the fish to come over it.

'Don't move it,' I warned. She didn't bother to answer – I guess she knew about that too.

At last we saw the golden brown fin above the water and the whole great curving back came into view, with its big shining scales; then the head lifted, showing the barbels trailing from the huge mouth.

It swam easily over the net and Jan went to lift it. Problem was, the fish was too heavy to raise on the end of the pole. I waded in to grip the pole closer to the net, and with water sloshing over the tops of my boots and Ken making anxious noises, we brought it in together.

After he had dislodged the hook from the wide, tough mouth he said, 'We'd better weigh it in the landing net,' so we hung the landing net itself on the balance after quickly unscrewing the heavier handle.

'Seven pounds six ounces,' Ken grunted modestly. 'Not bad.'

We let the great fish lie out on the flattened

rushes for a few moments, while we marvelled at the size and the power of it. We agreed that it was far too big to go in the keepnet for the rest of the day, so Ken lifted it carefully and held it steady in the water while it got its breath back.

When it was beginning to push to be free he released his slight hold. It hovered for a few seconds in the shallow water, as if testing its freedom, then gave one violent thrash, spraying water into our faces as if on purpose. When we looked again, it had gone.

Ken gave a deep sigh of satisfaction.

'Right then you two, beat that!' he said, picking out another cube of luncheon meat and getting ready to cast again.

'We'd have a job,' Jan said generously. 'Brilliant fish Ken,' and we went back to our rods to see what we could do. At least the fish were on the feed.

Soon after, I caught a small roach, then a couple more, all about ten centimetres long. For a while the swim went dead, then a really nice perch, about half a pound, came splashing into my net. Then I caught a perch so small that it was a wonder the maggot hadn't choked it. Even so, it had its tiny, spiky dorsal fin up to prick my finger on.

A couple of bleak followed, and another little roach. It was good to be catching, even if some didn't count, but I envied Jan when she was suddenly back in the action with a superb two pound chub.

After I'd been over to admire it she said she was hungry and fancied a stroll. Ken wouldn't leave his rod – or was too tactful – so the two of us scrambled up the bank and wandered off along the river above the weir.

It was quiet once we were away from the roaring water. The river was almost completely smooth and we perched on a grassy ledge to munch a sandwich.

A line of young swans, half brown and half white, came cruising past, with mum and dad at either end. Then Jan cried out as a kingfisher streaked below the overhanging branches on the far side.

'I love them!' Jan said fondly. 'You're not too bad either...'

We had a sandwichy snog at that and I forgot all about fishing. Jan didn't though, or not for long, anyway.

'Right,' she said, nearly shoving me in the river, 'now let's sort that Ken out!'

She jumped up.

'Watch out bream, here I come!'

Holding hands, and still stuffing sandwiches, we made our way back. Ken didn't even notice our return. He was locked in battle with another barbel and it was my turn to feel jealous as we helped him land it.

'Just under six pounds,' he announced. 'Not bad again. I think I'll go on the float now, and build up my numbers.'

I nearly said 'Bighead!' but I was in a good mood – and at least he wasn't feeling angry any more.

So we fished on through the afternoon. I wasn't doing very well at all, unlike Jan, if the regular squeaks (from her) and splashes (from the fish) were anything to go by.

I thought I'd switch to swim feeder, since it seemed to be working for her, but when I was half-way through setting up my quivertip rod I saw that she was going over to float fishing.

I put on a reel with three-pound line and took it straight through to a size twelve hook. I baited it with a worm and maggot cocktail, filled the swim-feed with maggots and cast out, hoping for a really big chub.

Absolutely nothing happened for ages, but I forced myself to sit back and wait. Jan had made her first cast after changing tackle, and her orange float, tip just showing, was circling quietly in the centre of the pool. As I looked, it dived, and a fine dace came flashing into her net. Within a moment she had cast again.

I glanced back at my rod, wishing now that I was still on the float, and saw the tip tremble, stop, then jerk impatiently.

I struck, but was disappointed to see right away that it was only a small roach coming in towards me.

But when it was no more than a rod's length out, right on the surface, the pike attacked.

It came heaving through the shallows, all eyes and teeth and driving fins. It took my roach, launching clean out of the water as it completed the upwards surge. And it was huge. I managed to flip the bail-arm open just in time to save the line from snapping.

While the pike ran with its prey, I desperately freed off the clutch, then when it stopped its run and lay dead still, as they sometimes do once the kill has been made, I shut the bail arm and quickly readjusted the clutch to what I hoped was a safe limit.

All the same, the fish was so big that I didn't think I had a hope of landing it, even if it didn't just spit the roach out anyway. But there I was, joined on to it for the time being, so I had no choice.

Jan was beside me by now, eyes sparkling.

'Go for it Dave,' she was urging. 'You've got to land it. It's a monster!'

Even Ken had left his rod and come down for a look.

'You'll be lucky,' he said. 'There's snags in the water. He's bound to go round something.'

Well, we waited and we waited. The pike waited too. In the end I tried giving cautious tugs on the line. No response.

'See what I mean,' Ken said. 'You're snagged already. No chance!' and he went back to his own fishing.

Jan was more encouraging. 'Keep at it, it's going to take a lot of patience,' she said, then she too went back to her rod.

'A lot of luck, more like,' I muttered, giving another tentative tug. But this time it worked. The pike took off and the action began. With the clutch screaming, it ran across the pool into deeper water, under the far bank. Just as I thought it was bound to snag in the tree roots, it responded to the pressure of the line and swerved to hurtle downstream.

I felt the line catch on some obstacle, but under the force of the run it tore free, slicing and bumping through old vegetation on the riverbed. Then it went dead still again.

It went on like that, running, then stopping, for so long that my shoulder began to ache. I thought of the small hook, and the knot I'd tied, and I wondered how much longer it could hold. But still I concentrated – backwinding at extreme pressures, taking line in whenever I could.

And still the big fish ran, and stopped, and tested out the force that was holding it.

I was vaguely aware of Ken and Jan, fishing on. Jan occasionally called encouragingly, but all my attention was absorbed in the long, long effort of working with the fish, yet against it, hoping that in the end tiredness would bring it to the bank.

I'd never experienced such a strange thing before. In a way I began to feel that I knew the fish; I could anticipate its next move and I treated it gently, not just to try to stop the knot or the line from giving way, but because I knew the fish. I liked it.

And at long last – they said afterwards that I'd been playing it for almost half an hour – I felt a difference.

The line began to rise in the water until my swim feeder was bobbing on the top. Then it came clear out and I caught a glimpse of a huge greeny brown back and a big fin. The fish swirled, creating a mini-whirlpool, and made a half-hearted run down river, before allowing itself to be drawn – very carefully – back towards where I stood, trembling with the final tension.

It did the same thing four or five more times,

and I couldn't see how the knot and the hook were standing up to the punishment. Even now, I knew that it could all suddenly turn to failure.

In the end I could hardly believe it was true when, rolling slightly from exhaustion, the great head and deep, long body came drifting, almost easily, towards me. It wasn't resisting at all now, just obeying the insistent pull of the line.

I fumbled around for the landing net, but my hands were shaking and I was afraid to look away from the fish in case it made one last burst for freedom.

'Jan,' I called from a dry throat.

'I'm here,' she said. And she was, too. I don't know how long she'd been standing at my shoulder, landing net ready.

Carefully she waded a little way in to meet the pike, and then she held the net steady, waiting. I was still terrified that at the last moment the fish would lunge, snap the line and be lost.

But the long, lean, predatory head glided calmly over the net and, choosing her moment, Jan lifted it just enough to ensure that most of the fish was safely in it, even though a fair length was still outside.

She went to lift the net higher, but the pole began to bend, and the net stayed half under water. The fish thrashed the tail part of its body that was in the air, and the net dipped right under.

We both felt panic, anticipating a leap and an escape, even now, but suddenly Ken came splashing past Jan, up to his thighs in the water, until he could grasp the net itself.

He lifted it and swung towards the shore in one movement, depositing net, fish and all, on the bank beside me.

The immense pike slid out of the net, onto the rushes, and I saw the hook, lodged behind one of the hundreds of needle teeth, fall free. There was no sign of the roach.

I was shaking all over, and embarrassed at the tears in my eyes. Jan put her arms round and hugged me.

'Brilliant,' she was saying. 'Brilliant. The best!'

Ken ran squelching back for his camera and we photographed the massive creature as it lay there. It looked like a prehistoric leftover, with its cold, inhuman eyes, and incredible killing-machine of a mouth. The body was so long it was hard to believe that such animals really did live in this quiet river.

When I was playing it, I had come to feel that I knew it, like a friend, but now I knew that I didn't know it at all. It came from a different universe from ours. It was wonderful to be able to look at it

and touch it, but it was alien to our lives – a mystery.

We slid as much of it as we could back into the landing net, keeping our hands well away from the terrible spiked mouth, and weighed it, net and all.

'You'll have to take off a bit for the net,' Ken said, 'but that's nineteen and a half pounds! Good fish Dave. I don't know how you did it.'

'I've never seen anything like it,' Jan breathed. 'You were amazing!'

Glowing with the praise, and beginning to get my strength back, I laid my rod beside the fish, to check the length. Later, when I measured the rod, I found that the fish was over a metre.

We stood round it for a minute or two, but then it began to flick its tail, as if it had had enough of being messed about. We lifted the landing net, all having a share, and lowered it into the water.

It was easy enough to let the fish float and withdraw the net from under it. We watched anxiously as it seemed about to roll over onto its back, but it made just enough effort to right itself

For a few moments it paused, the gills working more and more strongly. Next it gave a kind of shudder, all down its great length. Then, seemingly without effort, it glided smoothly down and away into darker, deeper water, leaving only a ripple washing round our feet.

'I enjoyed that!' came a cheerful voice from behind us. It was Jan's Gramp, back from Bristol. I don't know how long he'd been there, but then, I hadn't been aware of anything very much for the last half-hour.

He said he was in no hurry and we could carry on. Well, I wasn't capable of fishing any more, and the others seemed to feel it was a good note to end on. In any case, the light was fading and Ken was starting to shiver.

'Right,' said Jan. 'We know who's won 'fish of the day'. So who's got most fish? And who's got the biggest variety?'

We went up to Ken's net to see what he had. The two barbel had been released, of course, but he reached in, and as he lifted out the other fish and set them free we counted. There were half a dozen big gudgeon, five nice roach and four perch of around three-quarters of a pound each.

'Seventeen fish and four varieties,' Jan announced. 'Not bad, Ken. Now yours Dave.'

It was a good job I'd caught the pike because all I had were the one chub, a few small roach, a couple of perch and two gudgeon.

'Ten, plus the pike,' Jan announced. 'Now mine.'

Well, she stretched her keepnet out in the shallows and we stood and stared. I knew she'd been catching pretty solidly, but I hadn't realised just how good she'd been.

There were dozens of fish, shoulder to shoulder in a sinuous dark mass, the whole length of the net.

'What are they all?' Ken asked, well impressed.

She listed them.

'Lots of bream – I really hit a shoal for about half an hour before they went off; quite a few roach, perch, chub, dace, two baby barbel, four or five gudgeon, and a funny one that looks like a mixture of all the lot...'

'OK,' Ken said quite cheerfully. 'Dave's got fish of the day, and Jan wins both of the other classes – too many there to count. But I'm happy with my barbel.' He meant it too. Who wouldn't be!

Jan lowered the mouth of the net and it was great to see the fish, all undamaged, stream easily back out into the freedom of the river. Then she shook the net to dislodge a last little roach, and laughed with delight.

'Looks like you've had a successful day,' her Gramp said. 'Take your time. I'll go and sit in the car and read my paper.'

He went off towards the road and we stood for a moment, enjoying the peace and relaxation.

'Dave,' Jan said. 'Do you think my other Gramp can see us now?'

The water flowed gently past us and a skein of geese flew overhead on their way to the night's roost. The sunset cast an orange glow behind the trees. There were no other sounds than the soft thunder of the weir.

'I think he can,' I said. 'Heaven can't be far away.'

She hugged my arm.

'That's what I think too,' she said, and she got busy packing up her tackle.

I felt I was in a kind of a dream as I sorted out my gear. Everything had been so right. The place was lovely, with the weir and the pool and the Avon flowing away through the fields. There was Ken, a really good mate, and the fishing had been brilliant, especially that awesome pike.

And as we plodded, eventually, back along the field-edge towards the car, lugging our gear, tired but very content, I think I half guessed, even in those early days, that Jan had come to stay – even though she'd outmatched the two of us.

RETURNED

'Hi Dave. How's the fishing?'

At first I didn't recognise the voice on the phone. It had a sort of an Australian accent, which threw me, but then I guessed.

It was Ken, and the first time I'd spoken to him for about thirty years. Since those great times by the water, fifty years had gone flying by.

Fishing is always good, and those first times with Ken had been something special again. But some time after we left school he went to work in New Zealand, and stayed – his uncle had set up a business there – and the only contact we had was Christmas cards, usually with a fish on them somewhere.

This is why it was such a surprise that June day to realise I was actually talking to him again.

'Can we get together, Dave?' he was asking. 'I've come over in a hurry because Dad's ill. He's going on OK but he's had a bad time. I'll be up at the hospital 'til about seven. Are you free at all after that?'

'Come straight here,' I said. 'We'll make an evening of it. Jan'll be pleased.'

'That's fine,' Ken said. It'll be great to get together again. And I need to talk to you. See you soon after seven then.'

Jan came downstairs at that point.

'Who have you just invited?' she asked, with her usual smile.

'Ken,' I said. 'Ken York! He's in England and wants to see us. His Dad's ill. He sounded a bit odd...said he needs to talk to me...'

'I expect he's stressed over his Dad,' Jan said. 'And he probably doesn't know anyone here much, after all this time.'

'Yes, I expect that's it,' I said. 'What shall we feed him on...?'

He turned up as agreed, very tanned and even bigger than I remembered. He brought a bottle of wine, and flowers for Jan, and after getting used to each other looking a bit different at sixty-five than we did the last time we met, we had a great evening.

After all, we were still the same Jan and Ken and Dave as we always were.

At midnight, Jan went to bed and left us still talking. We started remembering the good times we'd had together – at school, and on the river banks.

We remembered the time we rescued Sodger from drowning, and another time when Ken turned round to find that a cow was just finishing off his sandwiches. I reminded him of the day when he got his wellies full of water and set fire to his socks trying to dry them. Then there was the time when a holiday boatman, going too fast, washed all our tackle into the river.

But after a while I realised that I was doing all the talking. A couple of times Ken started to speak, but stopped. Then, when I was in the middle of telling him how I caught a netful of big bream, when Jan and I were on holiday in Ireland, he interrupted me.

'Dave,' he said. 'That boy. Do you remember? The bare-footed one...'

Before I could answer he went on, speaking fast.

'I've never forgotten that evening. Hardly a day goes by now, but it comes into my mind. It's really spooked me. We never properly talked about it, did we. Why didn't we? Were we that scared?'

He paused, staring hard at me. I was surprised, but I knew what he meant.

'You do remember, don't you?' he asked.

I said, 'Of course I remember. I've wondered about it myself. I think it did scare us a bit – even though he wasn't anything to be afraid of. It was just all so weird...'

The whole memory was flooding back into my mind. The way the atmosphere seemed to change when the kid appeared out of nowhere. His old-fashioned clothes and speech. The remains of the little cottage. The red berries over the hearth, that glowed like sparks in the setting sun.

A shiver ran down my arms, just like it did that night, and I was standing there again, watching the wet print of a bare foot drying on the doorway flagstone.

'Is it still there,' Ken went on, 'after all these years? The fields, the river? It must all have changed.'

I told him it had survived. There hadn't been a motorway blasted through, or an industrial estate plastered over it. In fact, it was surprisingly like how he would remember. Jan and I often walked near there at weekends.

'Dave,' Ken said. 'I'm sorry to put this on you, but are you free tomorrow evening? I'm tied up 'til seven again. Could we go back there? I need to see it again, now it's so near. Perhaps that'll get it out of my head...exorcise it somehow. I know it sounds stupid – I shouldn't even be thinking about it with Dad ill – but would you mind?'

'Of course not,' I said. 'D'you want to fish?'

'No – I don't think so. Let's just go.'

So we agreed. Ken left, and I went to bed, full of disturbed thoughts and memories. It had never troubled me like it had Ken, but I had to admit that the odd experience had always lurked in the back of my mind.

And I never had gone back to that particular spot on the river – as nice as it was. That must mean something.

At half past seven the next evening I parked the car on a strip of gravel near the bridge and we made our way across the fields. The hedgerow where the old cottage had been was quite a mature wood now, where some tree planting had been done ages ago. Jan was at a meeting so it was just the two of us, like it used to be.

We walked through the soft June air without talking much. Ken was looking at sights he hadn't seen for more than half a lifetime. It was a beautiful evening. The edges of the field were full of flowers, and birds were still singing. I breathed in the warm scent and remembered the first time I had ever crossed that field.

Soon we were looking right over the wide, flat meadow that lay between us and the water. A hint of mist was already rising, blurring the distant scene.

Suddenly Ken stopped. He drew in a sharp breath and gripped my arm. I followed his stare and saw a movement over by the river. A small figure had come up on to the bank and then another joined it.

'It's only two kids fishing,' I said. 'It could be us. It's like looking back in time.' Then I got goose bumps and wished I hadn't said it.

Ken didn't respond. He was straining his eyes to see better. Slowly and quietly we moved forwards, our feet brushing the first traces of dew from the grass.

As we drew nearer the picture cleared. I was right in thinking it was two boys. They had rods and their heads were close together, studying something one of them was holding. There was a square blue tackle box by one of them.

Then one cast, followed by the other. We moved a little closer and their voices came to us, indistinct, but lively, and one laughed. I shivered, remembering a roach that flipped back in the river, and a laugh that took me by surprise.

Then the boy by the tackle box struck, and from the curve of his rod it was clear that he was playing something heavy. The other one scrambled down the bank out of sight, to come back up, clutching what looked like a big bream. The two of them crouched over it, admiring.

By now we were close enough to hear what they were saying.

'Wicked!' said one. 'Best I've ever seen.'

''Tis a good fat fish,' replied the other, and as my ears caught the sounds of that voice it was as if a giant fist crashed me, with one blow, fifty years into the past.

I shuddered from head to foot and I felt as cold as ice. My rigid neck muscles kept me staring and staring at the scene before me. At last I did manage to force my eyes away to glance at Ken, and I was amazed at what I saw. He was smiling – and nodding.

When I opened my mouth to try to say something he put his finger to his lips. We looked back at the boys who were so involved with their fishing that I felt as if we were invisible to them.

We saw the fish returned and another couple caught. We heard the exclamations of the boy with the tackle box, and the laughter and advice of the other. We saw the bulging sack bag on the grass, and the crooked rod, now lying across it.

Then Ken put his hand on my arm and made a gesture with his head to say that we should go.

As we moved towards the road, we both kept looking back to catch a last faint glimpse, but the rising mist was blurring the view more and more, and the voices were dwindling to a murmur.

When we reached the edge of the field, and they were quite beyond our sight, we stopped. I looked at Ken, trying to understand his mood, and hoping he could bring things back to normal somehow.

'I knew,' he said. 'Somehow I always knew. I just needed to be sure.'

That wasn't what I had been looking for. I tried to be rational.

'Ken,' I said, 'it couldn't be him. It's fifty years ago!'

'It was him,' Ken said, 'and you know it was. It's nothing to do with time...'

He was right, of course. It didn't make sense and it was quite impossible, but I knew he was right.

'Well,' I said at last,'if it was him, that other boy is having an evening he'll never forget. But are you sure...?'

'Oh yes,' Ken said, completely relaxed now. 'As soon as we set foot in the field. Would you believe, for fifty years I've had conversations with him in my head...All the questions we might have asked him. Didn't he ever grow up? What happened to him?...Wondering if we could have photographed him...'

'And now –' I began.

'Now all I want to do is just slip away quietly. I'm content, knowing he's still there...until his mother calls him home. I'll be happy every time I think of him...in our field, by our river...fishing forever!' Then, with a complete change of mood, he looked at me and grinned. 'Right Dave, I've still got a couple of days over here. If you'll lend me a rod tomorrow we could go after that roach of Sodger's. It must be a twenty pounder by this time. Jan'll come, won't she.'

Already my heart was thumping with excitement. Tomorrow morning, as the mist lifted, we'd be somewhere by the water, unreeling our lines, shotting our floats, baiting our hooks...and casting into the flowing stream.

Fishing...fishing forever...

There are many more great fishing books available from Merlin Unwin Books, 7 Corve Street, Ludlow, Shropshire SY8 1DB. You can find details of them on our website (www.merlinunwin.co.uk). Why not write or email (books@merlinunwin.co.uk) to ask us for an up-to-date list of our fishing books? Some books, which we think you may particularly like, are featured below:

A Passion for Angling
Chris Yates, Bob James & Hugh Miles

This is the bestselling book which accompanied the BBC TV series of the same name. Chris Yates and Bob James set out on a fishing adventure across Britain. They have some incredible days catching carp, perch, pike, salmon and trout and this book tells the story of them. The many fabulous colour photos in the book record Bob's amazing bag of 2lb roach, the brace of huge pike, the carp and barbel caught by Chris and many other unforgettable fishing episodes.

£16.99

The Secret Carp

Chris Yates

Chris Yates takes the reader with him to a mysterious carp lake where he stays for 24 hours in search of the huge fish it holds. This extraordinary tale of carp angling captures all that is so compulsive about the sport: the anticipation, the signs of the fish, the preparation of tackle and planning how to catch the fish. And finally the thrill of the take and drama of the fight. *The Times* described this as 'the fishing book of the year'.

£16.95

Falling in Again

Tales of an Incorrigible Angler

Chris Yates

A brilliant new collection of fishing stories from angling's master story-teller. Yates goes on expeditions for carp, barbel, chub, roach, pike, gudgeon and even bass. He looks for the carp lake of his dreams, is evicted from the River Mole, and dangles breadcrust for chub from an overhanging tree... These are great fishing tales, and as always Yates keeps on 'falling in again.'

£17.99

The Pocket Guide to Fishing Knots

Peter Owen

The step-by-step drawings in this new book show the fisherman how to tie 24 useful knots - for all types of fishing. This compact little reference work - ideal for packing into the fishing bag - has been designed to benefit *all* anglers: game, coarse and sea.

Peter Owen - an angler himself - has selected only those knots which, in his view, are reliable and best suited to modern line materials.

This is the clearest, most helpful book on the subject to date. It will be of value to beginners, but also to experienced anglers who may wish to try out some new knots, and break with old habits! £4.99

The Pursuit of Wild Trout

Mike Weaver

The perfect book for anyone wanting advice on flyfishing for trout in rivers. Full of colour photos of the fish, the rivers, tackle and flies and practical tips on rods, lines, leaders, etc. Mike Weaver is Chairman of the Wild Trout Society. £16.95

Bernard Venables

Illustrated Memoirs of a Fisherman

Bernard Venables

This richly illustrated memoir records the life and fishing adventures of one of this century's greatest anglers. Venables created the popular cartoon character Mr Crabtree.

£19.95